PRAISE FOR WELCOME TO HELL

"Billy Pratt wanders and wonders through the ruins of what is left of our civilization and provides poolside musings on the façade of what passes for human relationships in our atomized present day. With more than a helping of melancholy and longing for things which are now past, Pratt writes in the mold of Delicious Tacos midway through an existential crisis. Enjoy these Despairing Tacos." — Mencius Moldbugman, contributor to *Ending Bigly: The Many Fates of Donald Trump*

"This collection is, as they say, a mood; an elegy for lost Americana, a memory of a place you've never been. If seduction is getting lost in the incomparable alienage of the other, and writing is teasing out the universal from the particular, then Billy tries to capture a universal sense of feeling lost. You will be able to see how much he cares." — Zero HP Lovecraft, author of *The Gig Economy* and *God-Shaped Hole*

WELCOME TO HELL

"Bad" Billy Pratt

Sheridan, WY
Terror House Press
2021

Copyright © 2021 Terror House Press, LLC.

All rights reserved. No part of this book may be reproduced or utilized in any form or by any means (whether electronic or mechanical), including photocopying, recording, or by any information storage and retrieval system without the prior written permission of the publisher, except in the case of brief quotations embodied in critical reviews and certain other noncommercial uses permitted by copyright law.

This is a work of nonfiction. While all of the characters and events depicted in this book are real, names and identifying details have been changed.

ISBN 978-1-951897-51-2

EDITOR

Matt Forney (mattforney.com)

LAYOUT AND COVER DESIGN

Matt Lawrence (mattlawrence.net)

TERROR HOUSE PRESS, LLC

terrorhousepress.com

TABLE OF CONTENTS

Zenith (The Low Hum of a Blank Screen) ... 1
Chasing Ghosts ... 5
Chubby Set of Bones ... 9
Back to the Future ... 13
Suburbia ... 17
Nightcrawling ... 23
K I LL T O P AR T Y ... 27
Problem Glasses ... 31
Bamboozled ... 35
Never Called Me Back ... 37
Adventureland ... 41
On Writing and *The Pussy* (2016) ... 45
Heartbreak and *Big* (1988) ... 51
Authenticity and *The Cable Guy* (1996) ... 57
Underachievers ... 63
Defiance on the Road to Decay ... 67
Graduating College and "In the Bedroom" (2002) ... 73
Stoned at Walmart and "Being Johnny Tangle" (2006) ... 77
Elizabeth Warren and the Death of MTV ... 83
Success ... 89
Dawn of the Dead ... 95
2019 ... 99
This Space Between Us ... 103
Don't Fear the Reaper ... 109
Some Time Alone ... 113
Dating and Reality (Picnic, Lightning) ... 117
Better to Reign in Hell ... 121

Purity and Mayhem ··· 125
Eternal September ··· 129
The King of Hell ··· 133
Set it and Forget It ··· 137
You're Just Like Delicious Tacos ··························· 141
Ghostbusters 2 ··· 145
Jennifer Lost the War ······································ 149
Only Death is Real ·· 153
After Hours ··· 157
Endnotes ··· 161

"Hey, Mama, look at me, I'm on my way to the promised land…"

ZENITH (THE LOW HUM OF A BLANK SCREEN)[1]

"Run and tell all of the angels, this could take all night..."

Nancy had done her part by having a kid. Something anyone could point to as making her *accomplished enough;* anything on top of that is a victory lap. No one would fault her for keeping things quiet; drinks on the weekends, maybe a date, vacation time over the summer. This is how she eased into her forties, and there was nothing terribly wrong with it, even if her only wish were to politely color within the lines and walk away with a terrifically neat and tidy picture of a life well lived.

First time I had dated someone so incredibly *settled*—she even had a house to go along with the kid. Only a few years older than me, but it felt like decades. With my baseball cap turned slightly askew, I still think I'm a 25-year-old rock star with a full road ahead of me. This is the fantasy you indulge in when you've never chosen a path: you pretend that you still have choices, and that you could be smug about those boring types with their suburban homes and vacation clubs.

Only a few years older than me, but I called her my *old lady girlfriend*, for reasons that are more clear in retrospect. Maybe I needed a feeling of distance from how quiet things were for her; maybe I felt a degree of insecurity about how unsettled my own life was, as if dating her made me confront my own reality; sideways cap and rock-star fantasy be damned.

Maybe I felt the need for distance because this wasn't my life and it never could be; I was just filling in. Her Scott Weiland had checked out years ago; I was only a hired gun, her Jeff Gutt; let's do an album and a tour and call it a day. This wasn't my story, and the space between us made that fact immutable. This wasn't my story, something one of her friends explained to me on a drunken bar night—as if to skew my expectations—"She cares about you as a person, but you're not the love of her life."

This wasn't my story, and we had no reason to pretend it was. There was a comfort in understanding that it was *good enough*. It was functional. We got along. We had incredible sex. What else could one hope for in the land of the dead?

I didn't choose a path, so one was chosen for me, like I let the menu screen run for too long and the game booted up on its own. *Unsettled* is my path, and it ran diametrically opposed to hers. We were different people with different lives. She was a good kisser; we spent most of our time in the orbit of her bedroom—afterwards, she would talk about whatever cruise she had planned, and I'd talk about my writing.

She'd tell me that she didn't understand why I liked writing. She didn't understand why I bothered or what I was looking to get out of it; why I took it seriously, why I'd be so hard on myself over it, why I never thought it was good enough. I'd talk about the ideas I'd have for pieces—the frustration I felt in my attempts to bring them to the proper terms—and she'd stare blankly and tell me that she didn't *get it*, which I suppose was slightly more polite than telling me to shut the fuck up.

Nancy didn't see the value in any of this because it wasn't part of her world, a very tangible world of cause and effect. You work for long enough to cash in your tokens for a week in Florida. A localized world where you meet with friends at a pub and order an Uber for the way home. A world where you rest easy at night knowing that you had a kid, created meaning in what is inherently meaningless, and can enjoy the blank spaces that life will offer.

I don't sleep well at night, and I haven't for a long time. I'll often wake up with feelings of an unidentifiable, shapeless dread—a subtle haunting—which I can't immediately suss out the origins of, that will cause me to stand in my kitchen for several minutes, long after midnight, composing myself. These feelings were stronger when my life was a disaster, after my engagement and career blew up at the same time, when I had given up on *long-term planning*, when I had suicide as a potential endgame, where I'd go out with two middle fingers aimed at a world that's only betrayed me. This felt like being on fire, which had since been extinguished, and now the remaining embers caused a dull burn.

Writing is the pursuit of truth; this is what I'll say when asked why I write. Not all writers are genuinely pursuing truth, but they think they are and that counts, too. One can either pursue family or pursue truth. While it isn't necessary for those who pursue family to also pursue truth, the option is available; however, for one to eschew family, one *must* pursue truth. Nothing else matters, and every little bit of consumption distracts from this pursuit.

This is why you spend your time grinding away; this is why productivity is all that matters to you. This is why bouts of creative impotence keep you up at night. This is why you can't picture yourself settling into a week aboard a cruise ship or hidden away at some resort hotel in Mexico; the anxiety of spending time doing anything but turning eternal truth into art nauseates you. You're an intellectual alchemist—Henry fucking Frankenstein,[2] half-mad, looking at your best work and swearing you know what it feels like t*o be God*. Greatness lies just beyond your reach, but it's there and you can feel it. Even starting with nothing, you can take what's needed from your surroundings and make from it something more. On your best days, by anyone's judgement, you'd have to be considered clever.

You can make up for mistakes made along the way; time lost; hearts broken. You can stitch things together—make sense of what went wrong—bring meaning to what is inherently meaningless and condense things to their proper terms—where those around you can look past the mess you've made and only see how you've come to frame it—in terms that are brilliant and meaningful. You create beauty in meeting dead-end girls and having dead-end sex in dead-end relationships; this wasn't time wasted, this was time *making art*. This is what you tell yourself in your kitchen, in the middle of the night, as the clock ticks away, and this is the part you leave out when asked why you write.

CHASING GHOSTS

"And now I tell you openly: you have my heart, so don't hurt me…you're what I couldn't find…"

I've never experienced anything more ethereal than when our eyes met before homeroom. It couldn't have lasted more than a few seconds, but it hung in the air like an eternal sunrise. Nothing I've experienced since has matched this feeling; for only a moment, I stood before the face of God. Drug people lament the way it *used to be,* before things were cut with fillers, watered down, muddled, meaning progressively lost; purity replaced by mayhem, innocent experimentation escalating to candy-flipping handfuls.

The first moment you fall in love, the first semester at college, and you're popping pills at a party- throbbing waves of intensity. And you think you'll take that feeling with you, like you finally won the ring-toss at a carnival. This is your big pink elephant, and it's yours forever. You think it's going to feel that way every time with every girl, but every time you go back, there are more pieces missing. The fifth time through the haunted house at Adventureland and the plastic skeleton doesn't have the same resonance. You become the old, recluse pothead rolling his eyes at kids going on stoner adventures; paint chipping away, hardwood floors stained, crabgrass growing through the cracks of the cement.

Our first movie date and I get her a yellow plastic ring out of the quarter machine. Someday, Jessica, *someday.* It's not that it wasn't meant to be ironic, but that its irony was so genuine. In another life, we'd be married now; two kids, in a house with a two-car garage. Yard work on the weekends while she shuffles the kids between soccer practice and kung-fu classes. At night, we laugh over Chardonnay, remembering how Sister Eileen would catch us making out in the hallway and then try to embarrass me about it during math class. You don't realize how much that means until you can never have it again.

Pressing her against the wall when no one's looking, biting her neck and grabbing a breast. We never lost it, did we?

No one expected me to break up with her. She was gorgeous, but we drifted apart. The sun had finally set. Seeing her would only feel empty. It was an integrity move. I didn't like her anymore, and isn't that why people break up? Paint the house to burn it down. Allow the perfect to get in the way of the good. I'm the captain who's playing by the rules if shit goes down in the middle of the Atlantic. A modern, suburban samurai with an unbreakable will to do *what's right,* even to my own detriment.

***

In my mind, I'm Lou Reed. Life is performance art, and you never settle for less than authentic. When Reed walked away from the Velvet Underground, having produced some of the best music of the decade that no one gave a shit about, he took a job picking up garbage on the beach. "Lou fucking Reed collecting trash" is what David Bowie must have thought when he offered to produce a solo record, the incredible *Transformer* (1972), which provided Reed's only mainstream hit, "Walk on the Wild Side."

With unprecedented career momentum, Lou cashed-in with *Sally Can't Dance* (1974), a terrible record that hit commercially. This rather common dichotomy, an awful record that awful people with awful taste seem to like—something that wouldn't have even registered with a band like KISS[3]—tortured Reed. Feeling compromised, thinking his career couldn't be salvaged, he did what any self-obsessed person would do: he burned it all down. Releasing an album of pure noise, Reed attempted career suicide.

Metal Machine Music (1975) is nothing but guitar feedback; there is no melody, there is nothing enjoyable. Anyone who's said they've listened to the whole thing is either lying or retarded. Not only did putting out a self-destructive record take balls, but Lou even had the balls to make it a *double album;* one solid hour of screeching noise. If you're going down with the ship, you may as well sink the Titanic.

Lou didn't like his career anymore, so he broke up with it. It was an integrity move.

***

Even if she were gorgeous. Even if we were just hitting our sexual stride, where Friday nights were pizza and root beer, and fucking her on the floor of her living room. Even if she loved me with a teenage intensity they all say is bullshit—"you don't know what love is"—but like anything they've ever said, the polar opposite is true. The only real love is teenage love, and even if she were the only girl who would ever love me.

I called her one night and broke up with her.

I ran into her at a club just after our first year of college; she was in black fishnets. There was a dumb luck to her growing up in the late-90's, Hot Topic, suburban-shoppin-mall, glam rock aesthetic. A slender frame with big eyes, dark hair, and large breasts, Jessica was a grown-up Powerpuff Girl, the goth girlfriend you've always wanted. Back on the floor of her living room; her parents were on vacation. We never lost it, did we?

She tells me she loves me with a hopeful uncertainty. I say nothing. She starts to cry. I'm too drunk to leave, but it's time to go. Hands around the wheel; ten and two. Keep your eyes open and try to look straight. A half-hour home. Choke the vomit down; this train's not stopping.

She tells me she loves me, but she doesn't understand that even if she were gorgeous, this wasn't our time. This wasn't our story; we still had college parties to attend and hook-up culture to explore, meaningless flings and endless variety, experiences and experimentation, throbbing waves of intensity, possibilities expanding beyond the infinite. Full lives to lead. Where people don't marry young, an archaic, barbaric practice from prior generations who were *uneducated* and didn't understand the value in personal development and irresponsibility. Where people don't marry young, and those who do are *uncultured,* working-class losers, grease on their hands and a pregnant wife in the kitchen.

She tells me she loves me and I say nothing. I'm doing her a favor. We're better than that, baby. It was an integrity move.

CHUBBY SET OF BONES

"Crucify the insincere, tonight, tonight..."

Like buying Bitcoin for pennies, the peak time to meet a girl on the Internet came and went before you ever knew what you were losing. Before anyone would have thought to use a term like *early adopter,* a time so raw that it couldn't have been confined to language. Before they called it the "wild West." A time without shape or form.

Forget selfies, rewind past digital cameras; when scanners were still *emerging technology,* the most pressing question after "ASL" became finding out what she looked like. The description of her body would ignite the imagination. You'd never have guessed that this primitive fumbling would yield more honesty than digital pictures, 20 years later.

I knew I was in over my head when I heard Kristen's voice. She spoke with the easy confidence of beauty. I always came out of left field. The outsider art of trying to get laid. A puncher's chance, but give me enough time and I'll land a clean left hook. There was a crazy charm to this and Kristen picked up on it. She didn't know what to make of me, but she knew I was unlike anyone she'd ever met. I spoke with the easy confidence of insanity.

***

We met on the cusp of autumn turning cool, where the air feels heavy and frames the night for romance. Parked under the tracks, she tugged and tugged the sleeve of my sweatshirt until I was close enough; we made out to the sound of passing trains. She was the prettiest girl I'd ever kiss, when I thought kissing the girl meant riding off into the sunset. She *likes* you, with a capital "L"; you've slayed the dragon. The victorious boxer getting his gloves cut off; opponent unconscious on the mat. A time when it seemed natural to think your work was done and you've reached the end of the movie.

Kristen was the first girl I'd kiss after Jessica. She was the kind of girl who had every guy in the room gawking at her wherever we went; dark hair and large breasts. She was the hottest girl in the club out with a kid in a Misfits T-shirt. She would've never known I existed without the Internet, a realization I made concurrent to the feeling that I was in over my head. Had life progressed naturally, in a timeline without the interference of technology, I would have never been afforded these opportunities, but the human animal *adapts*. Seagulls at the beach learning to scavenge through garbage. First guy in the room to buy Bitcoin; meeting *local singles* in AOL chat rooms.

Our drama would only last a few weeks. A girl with disposable attention will expect constant hits of dopamine. Minor deviations—seconds fractured into milliseconds, moments less than ethereal, temporary loss of emotional faculties—will extinguish interest. I was too heavily invested to effectively compete. Her game playing was effortless, built into her muscle memory, unconscious reflexology, Anderson Silva dancing around Forrest Griffin. Patty Hearst with a machine gun—not getting the message, instituting my own torture—everything disconnected, symbols vacant of meaning—the less she wanted me, the more I needed her.

Like the drug dealer in an afterschool special, she gave me a taste and I was instantly hooked. This kind of emotional warfare would define all of my future relationships. I did my best to keep up. I wrote taunting poems accusing her of being spiritually dead and kind of fat (she wasn't) while implying that I was fucking another girl in her absence. When you can't compete, you try to win by disqualification; the others were inauthentic and insincere, they didn't understand truth and beauty, she didn't need them like you knew she needed you. This bought me a few more hookups, but I was ultimately out of my depth. Still, she'd remember the poems years later.

When you start down the road of emotional manipulation, you end up an addict. You'll never let a situation spiral out of your control again, but you start getting hot for the process as an unintended consequence.

Coming up with jabs and tuning into the subtle reactions that a girl thinks are hidden. When you find a sore, you pick at it. You'll end up getting off on this harder than you get off on sex.

Years later, I'd tell Abigail that she had *cute knees*. And she did; petite in stature, she had the thighs of a woman who had not yet borne children. The knees of a teenager, untouched by time. But when you play these games with a smart girl, you get called out on your bullshit, something that would make me smile. If you're smart enough to pick up on it, you deserve to win.

You like to break women down so that you could rebuild them in your own image, she'd tell me. Your compliments are backhanded; insults by omission. You want her confidence dependent on you, reliant on your permission. Her only source of dopamine: good feelings, self-esteem. You become her dealer and you want her hooked. You want to own her.

You want to own her and there's a magic to believing that ownership—permanency, *consistency*—is even something possible. That the acknowledgment of feelings had and moments shared will create an organic entity that may necessitate both parties active and present, but is also something so tangible that it can exist independently of either; talk of *our relationship* like an 18th century alchemist; Henry Frankenstein stitching together something beautiful and new, *creating life* out of thin air; us against the world; good times and bad, riding off into the sunset, writing your own story and getting to the end of the movie.

BACK TO THE FUTURE

"On Marty's right was dear old Mom, who was once very attractive and bright. Now, at 47, she was overweight, drank more than was good for her, and had more food on her plate than anyone else."

I wasn't trying to have sex with Christine, but I wasn't opposed to it. She was in town visiting from some far-off country where she had gotten a job teaching English, picked up a relationship, burnt through it, and came back to her hometown to regroup before doing it all again. She'd come back home for gift cards and praise, complementing her courageous and free spirit, to have a few parties in her honor—maybe hook up with some old flames—and leave before it all started feeling too familiar. I never left our hometown; I was neither courageous nor a free spirit.

We were the first generation to explore our late twenties as unmarried. As it turns out, this only extends adolescence, creates expectations that life won't likely meet, and gives you a handful of addictions to grapple with for the next decade. If you're lucky, you'll have your head screwed on by 40 and then spend the rest of your life playing catch-up like you're running out of time on a level of *Super Mario Bros.* (1985), the background music fast and anxious so you don't forget.

The first generation where men and women can *just be friends,* where the sexes aren't diametrically opposed, constantly playing out like Biff Tannen chasing Lorraine: the perpetual antagonist meeting the perpetually antagonized until one is stubborn enough to give in. Christine was coming over for drinks, and I knew that sometimes, men and women had sex, even as friends, even if I hadn't ever experienced that myself.

I'd had girlfriends, and I'd had dates, I'd had dates that turned into girlfriends, and dates that turned into sex, but never a friend with supposed benefits. While I knew what these benefits were, I wasn't exactly sure how they were secured. Nothing about a friendship screamed sex, that kind of dangerous, animalistic tension; this was more like a cocker spaniel[4] playdate.

But friends had sex—I was sure there was a precedent for this—and I wasn't opposed to having sex with Christine. Men don't waste time with women they don't vaguely want sex with, and this was probably the bulk of guys lining up to make plans with Christine.

It's not that she was ugly; she was just painfully average. Never the prettiest in any group photo she's taken, she had a kind of toothy smile and an uncharacteristically flat nose for an Irish girl. Perpetually 20 pounds overweight, but it usually "went to her chest," a luxury men don't have. We went to the same high school, and in another time and place it wouldn't have been such a far-off idea that we'd have married. The same kind of unremarkable, though not necessarily undesirable, aesthetics would've produced some equally average kids who'd have gone to the same school as us, played on the sports teams we were too cool to join, and gotten eventual office jobs, meeting their own unremarkable mates, and starting the process over again. Not bad at all, just *unremarkable*.[5]

Of course, Christine and I thought we were too special for that trajectory. It wasn't cool to marry young, and definitely uncool to have kids before *experiencing life,* as if having children were a death sentence. How else would you have these drunken nights, anyway?

We didn't have sex—that notion died fairly early in the evening—and it shocked me when she told me about the kind of guys who *were* having sex with her. Cool guys, athletic guys, rock band guys, frat guys, guys whom I'd have thought wouldn't waste their time on Christine, someone who was a vague "I guess if it *just happens*" type of notion for me. She'd spend more time talking about the ones who must've gotten her goat; they were always *little boys* with *small dicks*.

I didn't know it then, but I'd made the mistake of thinking men and women could be friends in the first place. Just like I was only hanging out with her because *you never know,* she wasn't really looking to have a genuine conversation with me. When she first gave me her phone number back in high school, my father sat me down, after overhearing one of our endless phone calls, to tell me that none of the girls that I was *just friends* with would ever want to be my *girlfriend,* and I still feel guilty for reacting like a total shit to what must have been a difficult conversation for him to have because I was fucking embarrassed…and just like always, she was using me as an audience to complain about boys who'd fuck her but not want to date her, while not wanting either with me. My father was right.

But, even if sex would have been vaguely welcome, it wasn't pressing; I genuinely thought we were old friends first and, and as single friends in their mid-twenties, we were talking shop about the complex sport of male/female relations. She brought up *small dicks,* so I had mentioned, in passing, that guys with small dicks should just match up with smaller women who have *smaller vaginas.*

Her face turned red, and she shouted, "All vaginas are the same size!"

***

Christine didn't end up marrying one of her Biffs. A few years later, she met her George McFly—an Asian boy with a nice smile—gained 30 pounds, and started having kids. Her last *great adventure,* she told me, the last time I'd probably ever talk to her, too; and I let those words settle into the atmosphere. I didn't want to screw Christine anymore, so there wasn't much reason to keep up the conversation.

SUBURBIA

"Whatever happened to all this season's losers of the year? Every time I'd got to thinking, where'd they disappear?"

There is no place I'd rather be than walking beside a well-groomed front lawn on a suburban street in mid-August. Late afternoon, when the sun is just beginning to set—tired from a long day's work—making its march toward the kind of warm hue that feels like a soft blanket enveloping your soul. The sound of distant lawnmowers and the scent of cut grass; really, to properly maintain the admiration and respect of your neighbors, twice per week is ideal for lawncare. American flags next to empty mailboxes. Dogs barking beside hamburgers on propane grills.

When you're in eighth grade, suburbia is your canvas. You burn things in the woods and throw eggs at houses. Hop fences and explore backyards. Stand atop a hill overlooking the town below and throw-up a double middle-finger.[6] You let the girls hang out with you and act like it's this *big deal* and if they're not cool enough they'll have to go home. You probably could have seen their tits had you been more socially adept. You'd be stargazing had there been stars to see.

There's a beautiful quiet to suburbia at night. I never wanted to live anywhere with a *nightlife;* I want the late-night streets to be cold and lifeless. I want to hear crickets between faint sounds of traffic imposing from the highway. I want to sit on the baseball bleachers of the local high school and look out into the vacant soccer field. I want to walk down Main Street, past the charming specialty shops who are closed for the night. The little hardware store that you visit to make a statement against big-name retail. The model train shop that you know stays open as a passion-project rather than a money-maker. "Art by Alison" with the ever-present sign on the door advertising *open classes, starting soon,* where good vibes are taught in equal proportion to artistic technique.

***

First time I heard from Christine in a long time. She knew I'd be somewhere close to the old neighborhood, a fact that I always felt needed defending when I saw her. Seeing Christine meant she was in a place between the panels of her comic book adventure; coming home was only transitional. It was between teaching English in Brazil and working at an orphanage in China. She considered working at a school in some African country, but then found out it was being set up by missionaries and felt this was too imposing on "organic African culture." Home was never a destination; it was a stopgap for gift cards and praise.

She'd always ask if I was happy with how things turned out. What a question. Where do you begin? "Well, not because I stuck around…not because I didn't go on these inauthentic, *pretentious* adventures…" Where do you begin explaining that we're living in Hell? That to a highly-trained eye, which I possess, there are major differences in the singles market of 2012 compared to the cursed singles market of the current year? How modern men are more disposable than ever…where you like your little fucking town and you never wanted to leave. Has she seen the little fucking art studio and the toy train shop? Does she not get that it's all so *fucking charming?*

Christine was pregnant. She was getting married. They were looking for a house. You'd think that, in a fair world, the country-hopping would come at the expense of long-term stability. That there would be a *cost to the experience;* this is what felt fair. Every time we'd catch up, there was a new story; the guy in the indie rock band out in Austin, the soccer player in Rio. But, not this time; this time she had met a lovely boy in Portland, where she ended up after the work visa expired in China—a "crazy story," I was assured—and now her next adventure was having a family. It sounded like a movie trailer.

You have these defensive moments, but they pass, and it's back to the empty soccer field at midnight with your notebook, making words into art.

***

My favorite movie, as a kid, was *Clue* (1985), so much that my parents got me a real-life singing telegram for my seventh birthday. No, I didn't get to kill him. Yes, I'm still unsure of how to properly respond to an adult singing to me. There was a line in the song about how much I loved watching the singing telegram get shot. I wonder how that made him feel.

I was obsessed with the *Clue* mansion, a gorgeous, authentic-looking Tudor with a classic black-and-white tiled kitchen. A study to provide the feeling of quiet solitude, even in a house brimming with life. A billiards room to swill brandy and smoke cigars while entertaining colleagues. A conservatory to enjoy the picturesque garden, leading to the partially-cultivated acreage of which your home overlooks. Secret passages and hidden rooms, candlesticks and daggers.

When you're a kid, you think anything's possible—even if your future is genetically etched into the hollows of time—but you're sold the lie of life as a big slot machine and everyone getting a turn. Line up three cherries and get a model wife and a million dollar home. It could happen *to you,* as if life is a movie that unfolds and branches out with a will of its own.

There's a premium to suburban authenticity. The most you'll ever get is to enjoy it from afar. Close your eyes and take in the cold December air, the taste of midnight. They say it's best to ignore what you can't have, to *hold it in disdain.* You'll never get the Lamborghini; Bitcoin was a plebeian fantasy. A day late and a dollar short on that, too; what else is new?

But walking past an old Tudor home, you can close your eyes for just a moment and pretend that it's your life; that it *could be* your life. Another round, another hand of cards; play it right this time. By the fireplace, under the arching roof, watching the wintry mix fall from the wooden-framed windows. The light switch on the wall is the kind with the two-buttons: true "pre-World War II" architecture.

Don't feel too badly; it was never gonna happen. You were never going to transcend the working class, even if yours is a job only made possible with multiple college degrees. There are comfortable dwellings for your type, but the architecture is different for reasons I refuse to accept. Middle class homes are "standard-issue life-boxes" set on small plots of land. There is no personality to a middle-class home in modern suburbia. If you want something unique and authentic, you'd better know that it comes with a hefty price tag attached. When you get back home, after taking in the crisp December air and admiring what you'll never have, you can sit by your electric fireplace and listen to "March of the Wooden Soldiers" on FM radio.

Sweet Jane's out with some other asshole, if you didn't already know; everyone becomes interchangeable eventually. Young love is the only true love, a fact you learn long after the wave's crashed and the tide's receded. You found tons of petty reasons to avoid a relationship with her, anyway. Too many buyers on the line when your phone still rang. Little things to nitpick. You leeched off of her like a vampire and now you sleep alone.

Growing up in suburbia engenders an obsession with minutia. The tendency toward authoring your own experiences with an iron fist, molding things until they're photogenic, often by sheer will. This desire has superseded what's practical and comfortable; all that matters is *perception control*.

When Alex moved to the city after graduate school, what you'd think was undesirable suddenly became *shabby chic*. The railroad-style apartment with few windows and impossibly hot summers was a self-imposed hardship to fondly remember. The stench of the street, awful at face value, carried with it a kind of *otherness* that was vacant in the sterile suburbs. Teenagers on bikes smoking pot and blasting music; this was *authentic*.

The engineers of suburbia would have thought he was fucking retarded. The suburbs were designed as an *escape* from the filth of the city, and only for the highly privileged. The idea for suburbia was for it to look as though a sprawling, well-groomed public park had sprouted beautiful homes. The transition between park and home was to be seamless—country living within reach of city convenience—a scenic middle ground between wilderness and civilization. The suburban zoning laws were to be strictly enforced; front lawns exist today due to laws preventing a homeowner from extending his home to the property line. The suburbs were meant to have a quiet dignity. Even the nicest areas of the city were *close enough* to slums; the suburbs could be beautifully segregated. Clean streets and quiet nights. Barking dogs and charcoal grills. American beauty.

***

She wasn't sure if she was ready for any of this, she tearfully confessed. I knew Christine better than she could fake it. The cool girl thing was a pose to get fucked by cool boys[7]; the country hopping was for Facebook. I can still close my eyes and remember the awkward girl on the transfer bus with the lisp and torn stockings. There was a comfort in my knowing who she really was, even if it was hard for her to remember. There was a reality below the surface and now she was afraid. She was afraid of what she was giving up. She was afraid of committing to the normalcy of family life, something she would inevitably view as defeat. Even if she had enough *crazy stories* for a lifetime, she'd be settling into what she railed against. She was back for good so her parents could help take care of the kid, along with their gift cards and praise.

***

The joke about growing up in suburbia is that there's nothing to do. If you weren't part of some highly-structured afterschool activity, like being on a sports team or writing for the school newspaper, there was a silent inertia pulling you toward destruction, like a suburban black hole. Interacting with the world as an emerging adolescent became a pissing contest in who could be the biggest prick. And once you figured out that *girls like assholes,* if you wanted any chance at getting a handjob, you'd better be the biggest prick in your neighborhood.

Kurt Cobain was the poster boy for growing up in suburbia. Touted as the voice of his generation, he spoke for *suburban youth.* His music reflected the emptiness familiar with any kid not on a sports team or taking piano lessons: the empty spaces of suburbia. You could buy a CD single of "Smells Like Teen Spirit" a few aisles away from Teen Spirit deodorant; there was a kind of murky egalitarianism of symbols rendering everything meaningless. Suburban youth only understood consumption—"here we are now, entertain us," Cobain snarled—and destruction.

Nirvana liked to destroy their equipment at the end of their set, a serious issue in their early days which gradually became more symbolic in direct proportion to the size of their bank account. This produced an intense focus on the present—there would be no tomorrow—but only as a consequence of having lost hope for the future. There was only today and today was to end in destruction, something every kid growing up in suburbia could understand.

Christine moved into a small apartment with her boyfriend and kid not too far from where she grew up: a new adventure indeed. The final iteration of our *cool girl* is a fat kindergarten teacher at a private school tiny enough to hire help without the appropriate college degrees. Now she posts awful Facebook memes like "I'm a Teacher…So What's Your Superpower?" This is how things were always going to settle for her, etched into the hollows of time. Ride the bus until the wheels come off and then hop out the emergency exit. When your culture never promised you a future, you take what you can get from the present and destroy the rest.[8]

NIGHTCRAWLING

"We were sure we'd never see an end to it all..."

There were others before her, but she was the first. I found Nikki on MySpace. She liked taking pictures; she was an early adopter of *digital photography*. Specialized in self-portraits; different angles, tight zoom.

You thought she was beautiful. A carbon copy of every girl-next-door you ever wanted in high school. This was your moment. You spent a year at the gym—hundreds of miles on the treadmill, throwing around dumbbells—training for this like Rocky Balboa looking for a comeback. You had girlfriends before—but this was your moment; experience, swagger, and fitness—you finally felt like a complete package. If out-of-shape guys date average girls, then fit guys have their pick; it's a logically valid equation.

It had been a year since Kasie, and there wasn't anything terribly wrong with her outside of her being terribly average. Friends teased about dating a *chubby girl;* fishnet stockings squeezing thighs with a *maybe-too-short* plaid skirt. She'd have meltdowns when she drank too much. There was a night at a club that anyone close to her nuclear epicenter will never forget, even 15 years later. But that wasn't the problem; you just thought you could do better.

People don't marry young anymore; before us lay a world where our value could be tested, refined, and maximized. We had time; we didn't need to settle.

You thought Nikki was crazy for showing up to your door the way she did. You thought she was fat. A modest waistline met with a big ass stuffed in maybe too-tight jeans. The prior decade's aesthetic of thin-with-large-breasts still hung in the air as ideal and Nikki existed as the polar opposite. You didn't know if she was intentionally deceptive with her pictures or if you were fool enough to deceive yourself.

She wanted sex, and we watched a movie. She was sweet. We'd keep in touch; just friends, because I was fit and charming and swagger and all that shit. I was too good to stick it in a fat girl; our values did not coalesce, our lines on the graph did not intersect. And even if I hadn't been with anyone since Kasie, a fat girl certainly wasn't going to be my starting point.

After a few months of nothing, I sent her a text. Since we weren't ever gonna be a thing, she loosened the veil; I was the only one she'd met who didn't fuck her. This shocked me; what desperate losers she must be meeting! Poor girl.

***

Kathryn wasn't ideal, but she was available and younger than Nikki, straight out of college and with a degree in English literature. I worked with her father, which was something she loved, getting off on the vaguely scandalous overtones of it all. Only a few years older, but to her, it was dating the teacher. Kathryn was average and Kathryn was boring, but meeting Kelly wasn't.

Kathryn introduced me to Kelly on a night at a pool hall. Recently dumped and needing to get out of the house, she tagged along. When Kathryn hit the bar for another drink, I joked with Kelly that we were all gonna end up in the backseat of my car, a physical impossibility that didn't seem to bother her when she told me that she'd be down but Kathryn *would never*.

Which was probably true, so we didn't bother asking. Kelly scribbled her address on a tiny piece of paper and snuck it in my hand as we said our goodbyes with the words "15 minutes" written above. 20 minutes later, we were in my backseat.

Kelly had a charming spunk to her. She was going to school to be a librarian and told me that her grandmother would buy her a new winter coat if she managed to lose 20 pounds. Seeing her was exciting at first but had diminishing returns as we drifted from forbidden to routine.

We couldn't date because Kathryn's father was a colleague in my English department, and even if Kathryn and I fizzled amicably, it would still be detrimental to date her best friend; that's what I told Kelly. But I didn't want to be tied down; long-term relationships leave post-traumatic scars. Three years in the clink. Like getting home from war and thinking you should re-enlist. Even if it makes sense, your body *won't let you;* that's what I told myself.

I didn't date Kelly because I thought I could do better, and I wasn't gonna wait around for her to get a new coat.

The gambler doubles down because he thinks the win streak will never end. Ace Frehley never stopped spending; why, when there's always another hit record? There isn't room to lose when you know how to win. So, the long months of nothing will be confusing at first, an adjustment period. Quiet reflection. You try to get used to rejection but never quite get there, like stepping into a cold shower; Wolverine and the claws coming out, puncturing knuckles, blood on his hands; it hurts every time. You text Nikki and get no answer.

You become the hungry coyote hoping to eat out of a dumpster. Lou Bloom stealing manhole covers to sell at 30 cents a pound. Your next meal isn't guaranteed; entirely possible you'll never eat again.

***

I met Lizzy a few months before she skipped town, a palette swap in place of something truly new, a different cast of characters but the same old problems. Instead of the purple-and-black ninja, now they're red-and-blue; she wanted a husband, but only met wolves; well fed, but when is anything ever enough?

Women are more pragmatic than men. They understand value. They'll cash in for a good enough deal. Left to their own devices, men get caught-up at the blackjack table, drunk on the possibility for more. Female charm is an evolutionary strategy to get men away from the casino, take the needle out of their fucking arm. Left to their own devices, men will run this lifestyle into the ground, and this is why we have women.

She lucked out when she met a big fat motherfucker who invented [REDACTED] and was filthy rich. Suddenly, her way of talking about relationships changed entirely. No longer framing things in terms of *passion* and *chemistry,* Lizzy had now "found her best friend" and "discovered what love really was," which I suppose sounded better than "he's fucking disgusting, but he's a multi-millionaire."

It was around this time that I met Marisa. I wasn't rich and she wasn't Lindsay Lohan, but a close enough approximation—the budget version—made it a love story. She was smart enough to get her claws in, like the raccoon who finds a way to open up the old pizza box while the others just stare. She got what she deserved. We both did.

It didn't work out with the fat motherfucker; maybe it was a little too good to be true, maybe he was just another wolf, but one who had come up with his own way to get it. Back to the drawing board, ground zero; she started reading books about being *brave,* just in case.

Years later, she managed to meet someone in-between hungry coyote and master wolf; tall and weathered, overweight with high school sports, always good for a few stories on a Friday night. If things were different, this is whom she'd have married out of high school: two kids, a two-car garage, yard work, soccer practice, kung-fu classes; holiday duties on the path to grandchildren.

She took the long way around, but she didn't time the market right. She had to catch a falling knife, and this is where she ended up, knuckles punctured, hands bloody. For Valentine's Day, he bought her a pair of designer shoes with a note attached: "A reminder to never settle for anything less than what you're worth…"

As if she didn't already know.

KILL TO PARTY

"'Cause we came here to set this party off right, let's bounce tonight. And if they don't let us in through the front, we'll come through the side."

Marisa had me drive her to her mother's apartment so she could steal money, behavior I never endorsed outright, but I'd be lying if I said I wasn't complacent, an accomplice, if we were to be arrested, which we wouldn't be; her mother was a dingbat. She'd keep loose cash in the drawer next to her bed, and every few weeks, Marisa would dip into it like a broken ATM. Hundreds of dollars missing; thousands over time. Her mother had alimony coming in from Marisa's lawyer father: when shit hits the fan, everyone becomes a thief.

She'd take enough to get a half-ounce from our dealer and have some left over to pick up dinner. Sitting next to a Family Dollar listening to "I'm Waiting for the Man." He'd text that he was "just pulling in to the parking lot" and show up an hour later; he knew you weren't going anywhere.

Brought a bagel sandwich and bag of chips back with me, the indie label, kettle-cooked kind that you pay a dollar more for and is more heavily saturated in a higher quality oil- safflower, which is less likely to cause heart disease, something I can only appreciate in retrospect.

We'd get high and watch the Casey Anthony trial.[9]

Casey had a luminous screen presence. She had an emotional range that Hollywood starlets had to envy, that corporate types spent late nights trying to come up with ways to exploit for the millions she'd be worth if only the public found their method semi-palatable. They knew there'd be backlash, but some amount of that is a good thing. With too much, heads roll and jobs are lost. Finding a way to use Casey was like dismantling an atomic bomb, but with rewards high enough to make solving the riddle worth the risk.

She had an understated sexuality that was ever-present. Casey was beautiful—dark hair and large breasts—with the disheveled look of a woman in need. Part of you wanted to save her, part wanted to punish her, emotions that somehow co-existed in an intoxicating swirl. She killed her daughter for cheap sex—she was lost, she was overwhelmed, she was scared—but you'd feel comfortable pulling her hair until she cried, until she begged for forgiveness, which you'd reluctantly grant and she'd be forever grateful. She'd love you.

Her story existed at the intersection between moral condemnation and empathy. How could a progressive culture rightfully find outrage in any of this while using "health care" as an awful nomenclature, something that even the most ardent baby-killers roll their eyes at behind closed doors… but you were still able to get that fuzzy feeling in the back of your skull as Nancy Grace barked about the monstrous Casey Anthony, with her dark hair and big tits, as you finished your blunt just past noon and fucked your hormonally-altered fiancée on your broken black couch.

Another wonder of the modern world—birth control—she couldn't get pregnant. Nature disrupted by science, sex detached from meaning. She'd let you look at bikini pictures of her old sorority sisters posted in private Facebook groups on her MacBook Pro as you fucked her, which you thought was hot. Take every situation to its peak: push every sensory experience to its breaking point with drugs and tech and food. This was the future we deserved; the organic tension of our first kiss felt distant and obsolete. Everything escalating to parody—she's blowing you as you talk to camgirls, you're watching Carmella Bing get fucked while she uses her industrial-grade Hitachi Magic Wand to get off—next she'll need a chainsaw. This was life's purpose: you kill to party.

After things fell apart, I'd tell people that I only *thought* I was in love with Marisa. That I was clearly wrong, that somehow love is an objective truth that we haven't quite developed a blood test for yet, and it's something that only exists in its eternal form, written in all caps and bold type.

But there were momentary glimpses and flashes, like feeling the tingles of an acid trip peaking, where things couldn't be described with anything less than capital letters and bold type. Sitting on my couch, well past midnight, emotions swirling with the force of a Gravitron spinning at Adventureland, dangerous enough rattling where you could rightfully close your eyes and believe you'd take off into outer space, suspension of disbelief not needed. Yes, I want to marry you. Her tears came harder than a chainsaw-induced orgasm. This was our moment; private and meaningful. Let's keep it a secret. Let's build toward it and earn it. No ring, not yet; just know that I'm in love with you, and I want this more than anything, and I'm serious.

But she was engaged now. She had to tell her parents. Just her parents, who wanted to know why she didn't have a ring. They didn't understand private and meaningful, words seemingly not in their vocabulary. If he wants to marry you, he'll need to pay your bills, this was more their speed. I picked out eBay's finest; $149, postage paid. A token, which her mother rejected, and if I wasn't going to *do the right thing,* she'd take Marisa out ring-shopping herself and send me the bill. Opening non-stick cookware at the engagement party; how thoughtful, thank you. My parents, or anyone else even remotely related to me? Well, they couldn't make it…

If there were luck in any of this, it was that it all fell apart before I could render the first payment. Marisa has lost her job, too—something about a boy with an emotional disability getting loose on her watch, running through the neighborhood shirtless, found urinating on an herb garden—which wasn't exactly her fault, but it didn't matter. You're staring at the chessboard and you don't want to concede defeat, but you don't see an apparent next move, so the trick is to take as much time as you can between turns.

I'll never forget the night we met. The moment I noticed her. The kind of full-body electricity you feel when you first get a look at someone you're inexplicably drawn to, as if you've found a way to tap into a hidden wavelength making you physically attuned to something you don't immediately understand, but if you close your eyes and let the current take you, you'll end up being carried off by invisible forces in the direction of all that is beautiful and true.

I thought she was beautiful, the only girl I've dated who I consistently jacked off to throughout the entire relationship. The actress who played Punky Brewster grew-up to look nothing like Punky Brewster, but if she had, she'd have looked like Marisa. Freckles and big brown eyes. A childlike naiveté that bordered on stupidity; a mystery that never needed closer examination, one that could just be. Like everything she did that was pushed to its breaking point, she was always on the far-end of any emotion, always emoting with screeching intensity. Up all night on ecstasy, navigating bouts of crying, fending off bouts of screaming, intense bouts of sexuality.

There wasn't a next move to make, only moments where I knew things had to end. Moments that I wanted to soak-in and crystallize, that I wanted to hang in suspended animation and expand far out into the galaxy. My parents were healthy. My dog was alive. If I got stoned enough, I wouldn't have to think about the mess I'd made, and at my weakest, I'd rather have ridden the flaming balloon down to a fiery heap rather than figure out how to pull myself out of the grave I had dug.

And one Sunday morning, I woke up and told her it was over.

PROBLEM GLASSES

We were somewhere around our second bottle of wine when I made the startling realization that Amy's unexpected British accent had faded into something more typical and American. Picking her up that night for drinks at the Reptile Zoo, I told her I wasn't expecting a British accent. She asked what I was expecting, and I didn't have a good answer. You exchange a few messages with a girl on OkCupid and agree to meet for drinks; what is there to expect?

You're there because your perceived value matched her barest threshold—stripped to its core through years of careful revision; weathering her expectations down to the essentials that she would have scoffed at as a younger woman—grade-D, but edible, meat—*but edible,* the part you'd like to emphasize.

She's there because she wrote back.

But it was when the accent disappeared entirely that I realized the true depth of the situation: Amy's out with me because she's a fucking lunatic. The damaged pair of Air Jordans—manufacturer's defect—looks okay in pictures, but get up close and you'll know why they're on clearance. And I'm the stupid motherfucker who likes that kind of thing, the normal girls are *boring* type; I want the curve ball, the crazy girl. I want the hyper-emotional; I want the bizarre. So, of course, the accent disappearing entirely from a girl who wonders why I think it's funny that she's "never been to Europe" is right up my alley.

When the bill comes, I ask Amy how much she's gonna throw in and she tells me she didn't bring any money. This was very funny to her. The accent was back. Son of a bitch.

As a girl, if you're not gonna pay, this is how to do it. None of that passive-aggressive shit; false offers through gritted teeth. Say you don't have money and think it's all a big laugh. She got me there. Amy says something like, "Well, do you want to fuck me or not?"

I say "no," and we leave. "No" is always the right answer, if you didn't already know that. That's the game. The game is sub-textual. Your job is to frustrate and confuse. This makes Amy whine about always getting what she wants and how men *don't say no* to her. She continues to spout gibberish. I allow it. This is funny to me. Always say "no." Women don't understand "no."

We get back to my apartment, and Amy wants to be fucked. I concede. My refusal to wear a condom displays my dominance; not that Amy had asked. She demands silence as she climbs on top; this is the only way I'll cum, she tells me. Fucking in silence, thoughts drifting. Don't move too much, she insists, it might take a while. This is what people kill and die for.

The new American dream. Gone are the days of marrying young. Our stock is bred for hedonistic exploration. *Gotta pump those numbers up.* Someday in the distant future, you'll hit a threshold, arbitrary to others, but a number deeply significant to you. One that eases the mind; that you've *had enough,* wild oats sown. There may not be new land to explore, flags to bury in virgin soil, but enough penetration and you can think you're a conqueror. An ego large enough to effectively manage a long-term relationship, using every bit of knowledge you've picked up along the way to help guide you, even if most of it is horrifying. That's the plan, if you could manage to stomach it; or maybe just ride the Hindenburg down to its destiny. Marriage is a bad contract, anyway; odds skewed toward the house, signed under duress; *don't you love me?* An entire generation of men in hiding, refugees from modernity. Horatio Alger snorting the last remnants of the sexual revolution on the way down with the ship.

Amy wants to stay over and I say "no." No. Women don't understand "no."

And in a flash, reality hits hard. This was too heavy for me to handle at 3 a.m. on a Monday morning. I was confused, paralyzed with horror, and would only agree to deal with my new reality in terms of fantasy: an analogy. What happens when Batman ends up in bed with the Joker? It sounded like a riddle. I had made a grave error in judgment.

I didn't think much of her asking me to retrieve her glasses after sex. She wanted to collect herself, this much was clear, but it was when I got a better look at the particular *pair of glasses that* I felt a deep sense of dread. The dark reality of the situation; I had a goddamn pair of problem glasses pointed straight at my head and the fucker was cocked and loaded. How could I not have noticed? I decide to slow down, to massage things. Let's explore the issue. She seemed upset; we can talk. Amy was a therapist; she's a *professional*. I asked her what her major was in college and she said women's studies. Was this for real? Was I dreaming? I had read about this kind of thing on the Internet, but I didn't think it could *actually happen* to me. Amy knew what she was saying; she had a *very deliberate grin*, I was sure.

I was too smug to let her stay over. I wanted to think it was all insignificant. She was like an angry dog, and I couldn't let my fear show. I had to be pack leader. On the car ride taking her home, she mentioned a friend who said she had been raped because her boyfriend fucked her and then broke up with her; a misalignment of personal goals, an informal verbal contract broken. This was rape, she explained. Son of a bitch. She got me again. Women don't understand the word "no."[10]

BAMBOOZLED

Even if the dire unavailability of parking in Jeanette's neighborhood had made the task of meeting her at her apartment for sex seem daunting, only minimally rewarding, I always had a thing for girls who looked like the nerdy Chipette, and this fact added a feeling of urgency to a situation marred with inevitable difficulty. Parking matters; inadequate parking is as off-putting as a bridge or toll, and I distinctly remember cursing the wind on an early August morning in 2006, drunk out of my skull, taking the parkway home because I was forced by law to relinquish my hard-fought spot, as per alternate side rules, and couldn't find a new one anywhere.

How would I have explained this to a dutiful officer of the law? Would he have been so kind as to understand the inadequacies of parking in that godforsaken asshole neighborhood?

Luckily, my intoxicated journey was cunningly executed without police intervention, but the scars remained, and while I would have thought that no amount of implied sex was worth dealing with this asshole neighborhood again, she looked like the goddamn chipmunk, so I felt compelled to piss in the wind and live out every Saturday morning fantasy I had clumsily composed in 1986.

Parking wasn't as arduous as imagined, but when I got to her apartment, I immediately picked up on her game: she bamboozled me.

She met me at the door and suggested we get dinner. Yeah, that's cute. It was only twelve hours prior that I had the Chipette squealing like a pig over the phone. Phone sex is a lost art.

You simply must come over and watch the fireworks, she told me. It was the Fourth of July. People would be out in the country having the kind of picnics that you only see on TV, at public parks with rusty, foil-covered grills.

If there was ever a time to find parking, this was it.

But it was a serious case of bamboozlement. I declined the dinner suggestion, which was certainly the correct course of action. You don't negotiate with a terrorist. I should have found a way out then, really, but the perceived effort in parking lent a contrived gravitas to the situation. Even still, staying was the wrong move to make.

We go for drinks and I pay. She wants this to be transactional; I concede. The law of the jungle is self-perceived value; violent interactions, verbal warfare, jockeying for position. Find yourself on the losing end of baseline adequacy, falling shy of meeting her inflated expectations, and she'll find a way for you to make up the difference: pay for pussy. No price posted. How are your negotiating skills? Put in a bid and hope for the best.

One drink.

Rejected. She wants a table. She wants dinner. You just *have to* try their Yoshi Tatsu spring rolls, she says. An appetizer, of course. Her drinks keep coming. Hayabusa's Exploding Anus for dessert.

When the bill comes, I have her pay for what she ordered.

She's shocked. She's livid. She's having a low-key, passive-aggressive fit.

Her attempt at a sexual bait-and-switch had failed. Turns out her pussy wasn't worth a $100 tab at the Samurai King. Back to reality. Maybe next time I'll be invited up, she says through gritted teeth.

NEVER CALLED ME BACK

"Some wine, some wine, she'll never decline some wine. She sees her ship is sinking so she's drinking all the time..."

Things just didn't go as planned, she told me, her face stained with tears. I knew she was talking about me; I was never part of the plan. She was naked and crying, something that would've turned me on, but I wanted to be there for her. It just wasn't in your cards, baby. I thought this was comforting. Confront reality like a stoic; always have a love of fate. The stars brought us together, baby—your life crushed by divorce, my eternal adolescence—if that isn't a love story, what is?

She swore she didn't drink at work, but she called this her *downward spiral*, so I always wondered. She'd get nervous when it was closing time at the liquor store and she was running out of wine. By three in the morning, she'd tell me she loved me.

I dismissed this as drunk talk. I knew she'd never remember. It felt vapid. This wasn't love, this was *mind-blowing chemistry,* code that girls on dating sites use for "hot sex"; her face would blush with orgasm. This was a momentary connection so deep that the coalescence of energy between us felt tangible. Even if it were only temporary, the reality of it carried a gravity so strong it held us to the bed. And even if she were only a year older than me, she was tuned into a frequency that I couldn't yet understand.

We were together because her husband left her. She had "daddy issues"; he was twenty years older. You'd think that would buy loyalty, but not this time. When I wasn't with her, she'd get drunk and watch her wedding video. You end up with people because their trajectory matches your own. Her line going down the graph to the left met with mine going up to the right. We are not parallel lines; we intersect. I was good enough to meet a recently divorced, alcoholic lawyer bent on self-destruction.

In my "unemployed and laughing about it" phase—a designation sadly not available on dating app profiles—my options were wide open. Women love the unemployed asshole. Everything in Hell is the opposite of what you think it should be. If you want to get laid, quit your job and message 30 women at 2AM; you'll be surprised at what you find.

I liked Abigail. She was cute and Irish; dark hair and large breasts. Vulnerable and she didn't bother to hide it. Men like vulnerability because it reinforces their identity as masculine. No one wants a strong woman. I romanticize broken women to make sense of my own choices. Their failures bring comfort to my own. We are the same, trying to make due in a toxic world. Broken women make for better stories, anyway. Years later, you can have a blog where you share these stories as a way to craft a narrative about your own life. You need this because these stories are all you have.

She'd say "it's an escape from mistakes that we make" with a smile before finishing her glass. She was talking about me again. Maybe Abigail was my *crazy summer fling*—where we'd wander the streets of her neighborhood at midnight and make out under the stars, laughing at anyone who didn't get the joke—but I was something different to her. I was part of her downward spiral.

"Oh Billy, if and only if…" she'd say with regret. Lawyers tell jokes rooted in symbolic logic, a class we'd both taken in college. *If and only if* because it was never meant to be; it was doomed from the beginning. We were on borrowed time, the eye of the storm before our lines on the graph separated for good. Our trajectories were never destiny.

She'd get drunk and tell me she loved me because she understood that love didn't exist outside of momentary glimpses and flashes. When you're sold love as a verbal contract, you'll have learned your lesson by the fire sale. You can marry your high school sweetheart and never know the difference or meet a vampire and get taken over the coals. In a cold world, people take what they can get and move on. People are flawed, people are selfish. He wasn't the man she thought she was marrying; he turned out to be something different. He sucked her blood until there was nothing left and then disappeared into the night. He left her dead inside.

But during these moments, I existed as her salvation and she loved me for it. This was love without expectation, love without narrative. We didn't need to pretend that it was something more than it was. Love is a precious moment where the energy in the room is so urgent that it can't help but be labeled. If you think love is anything more, I'll meet you at the fire sale.[11]

She'd get drunk and tell me to cum inside her. I never would, which was only the right answer depending on your perspective. Days later, she'd have her kitchen table lined with over-the-counter pregnancy tests. I couldn't tell if she was disappointed by the results. It just wasn't in our cards, baby.

Every summer has to end, even if you don't want to let it go. The end of August, lying naked in her bed; we never could escape its gravitational pull. She gets a phone call and excuses herself. 20 minutes later, she's crying in the kitchen. It's the guy she's seeing when she isn't with me. He's on his way over to kick my ass. She's sorry, she tells me. Downward spiral, I say. We share a smile. I give her a hug.

I'd never hear from her again.

ADVENTURELAND

"If you're gonna scream, scream with me. Moments like these never last."

I ended up with the plaid button-down because I needed a nice shirt to wear on dates; I was single again and recently set up a new OkCupid profile. I had found success on that platform in the past, although it felt like a thousand lifetimes ago when I was dating the daughter of a colleague in my English department while screwing her best friend on the side. All through the magic of online dating, but stay in a lecherous, testosterone-sapping relationship long enough and all you've learned gets lost to time; too many Diet Cokes in BPA-laden plastic cups at Friday's, too much time spent in front of network television, an unwilling prisoner of your girlfriend's viewing habits. Why are women obsessed with TV? Modern relationships should carry a warning label.

Women like preppy men, a friend's girlfriend had told me. Read their profiles and find something you have in common. "Mutual interests." Perhaps your values will coalesce. Women in their thirties are different, she said; you can't talk to them like everything is just sex. They want a caring, intelligent man. They're over their *asshole phase*.

Years later, I had the same plaid shirt laid out on my bed. Three months into dating Jennifer and suddenly I was on the losing end, playing catch up, trying to stitch things together. I needed her to see me again. One date would change things; a real date. Something we hadn't done. You could have convinced her that I didn't exist outside of my apartment because she had never seen me anywhere else. From Plenty of Fish to my front door, a short stop for phone calls in between; I guess I'm old-fashioned.

Plenty of Fish because OkCupid has too many pseudo-intellectuals; a serious misalignment between the lies we tell ourselves and reality. Girls who believe they are what they're not. Expectations derived from fantasy. Women on Plenty of Fish have experienced life's bitter winter. They know disappointment. They're looking for a man with a car and a job; the latter, of course, is optional.

Do it long enough and you get hot for the process, like a junkie with a head buzz just looking at the bag. She'll tell you that she doesn't send *those kinds of pictures,* but this is never true. Getting her older nudes is a victory, but having her take new pictures is a conquest. Big tits look their best in white tank tops (spaghetti straps, not a wife-beater), braless with hard, poking nipples. You want her in a thong, but specifically a G-string; strings on the side that press into her hips. This is important.

The pictures are less important than the fact that she did what you asked. The high comes from control. You don't bother jacking off to them, but you keep them to fluff your ego. Like her enough and you invite her to your place; another bit of compliance that's hotter than the sex you're going to end up having.

Only that wasn't the case with Jennifer. Every girl will tell you she gives the best head, an adorable white lie that you appreciate for the intentions, but Jennifer wasn't kidding. Sex with her became addictive. She got off on your control. No one had pushed her like you did; you enjoyed watching her squirm. When you play the game long enough, you can pick apart exactly what gets you hot: *honesty.* In a world of performance, you get off on the genuine. You want her to drop her guard. Destroy her ego. Show you who she really is beyond the false-self she projects. This is true submission, not the silly role playing that people take for dominance. You don't wait for a woman to tell you that she loves you; you look into her eyes and make her say it. Jennifer played these games with me, skating such a fine line between fantasy and reality that it was easy to get lost. Make her tell you she loves you for long enough and one of you is going to start believing it. Then one night, I maybe pushed too hard and she told me about the other guy she was seeing. Check.

If you aren't exclusive, she's seeing someone else, too. That's the reality of living in Hell. She had gotten me. This is the kind of blowback you get from making a woman say "I'm just a fat slut" during sex. Try it and you'll cum harder than you ever have before, but don't let her change the verbiage; *just* is important because it's reductionary. She needs to know that she's nothing more, at least in that moment, the moment your values coalesce. If she adds words like *I guess* or *kind of,* this means you hit a nerve, like striking gold, and suddenly getting her to say it becomes ten times hotter.

But this is a dangerous game, and even if she cums just as hard as you in the moment, she's going to hate you a little bit later on, no matter how many times you get her to say otherwise. Jennifer was fucking someone else, some guy she went to high school with, and used this as a jab at my ego, something which was unwittingly welcome. No false-self here; I pushed her to reveal the reality of the *single girl*—a perpetual 1970's key party—and we wouldn't need to pretend otherwise. She had gotten me, this was true, so I told her about Alison. She didn't like that. Check.

I didn't meet Alison on Plenty of Fish; I met her on Craigslist. Before they stopped hosting personal ads, a secret of the universe was that you could find much hotter girls on Craigslist, with a well-written ad, than any of the online dating apps. Leave your ad up and watch the replies slowly roll in; this was the passive income of Internet dating. Alison was a decade younger than Jennifer, with blonde hair and a modest bust; not necessarily my type, but with a girl under 25, who really cares? The irony is that I liked Jennifer more, of course; after all, this isn't about Alison, but like hell I wasn't gonna use her as collateral. When Jennifer tried to ratchet the game by daring to mention details, I pushed harder by leaving Alison's hairclip and necklace, mistakenly left at my apartment, on an end-table for Jennifer to find…and I won that round, too.

Like all victories, though, this was short-lived. The empire eventually strikes back. The true loser in a modern relationship is the one who takes it too seriously; an inherent falsehood, they're parody at best. My mistake was deciding that I wanted to do things right with Jennifer, but you don't politely ask to step off a runaway train. It's not for you to decide when the game is over. In one of those Alanis Morissette moments, the day I cut things off with Alison—seeing her had gotten stale anyway—to get serious with Jennifer—because I was falling for her—was the day she told me that she had met up with one of her Tinder matches. Tall with a big dick. Worked at a gym; she met him there and fucked on the massage table.

More blowback from the hairclip. Maybe I overdid it with that one. Isn't it ironic, dontcha think?

Like a wounded animal ready to die fighting, I didn't choose flight. I spent the next week berating her over text, telling her eternal truths that have become obscured by a modern world too happy to lie. Men don't think much of women who are easy sex. If she didn't already know that, she got to hear it 3,000 times. And it made me hot. I get off on being mean. The angry voicemails, cursing me for not picking up, followed by long messages of crying and begging. Her pleas for forgiveness. Her profuse apologies; she'd do anything to fix things. I'd get a head rush just seeing her name pop on my phone at work. This was a million times sexier than the world's hottest porn.

I'd like to think she planned the rest; clinch her victory and ride off into the sunset knowing she beat the asshole; just a fat slut? Not this time… but I know that isn't how it happened. Women are less principled than people think; they follow the tide and drift with the wind. Your actions rarely dictate their behavior; they'll either put up with you or they've found a better deal. A week later, we had the hottest sex of our entire run. All of the tension had led to a crescendo that exploded like a spear impaling a lightning bolt, a thousand atomic bombs exploding on my broken black leather couch.

Two weeks later, she's on the phone and I'm begging to see her. Let's meet at the beach. Find a bench and watch the tide roll in. Make out like it's our first kiss. No, she told me. She met someone else. Another guy from high school, one she'd never have considered dating when she was gorgeous and young, but like incubating in a pod, he emerged at 35, maybe not any better looking, but a doctor with a sports car, and someone who wouldn't make her *feel like shit about herself.*

But we were in love, I told her…before realizing I was alone in that sentiment. Say it enough and one of you is going to start believing it. Our values did not coalesce.

Checkmate.

ON WRITING AND *THE PUSSY* (2016)

"One time a thing occurred to me: what's real and what's for sale?"

When asked for writing advice, Delicious Tacos likes to keep things simple: get up early, every morning, and write. And there's something to that—the foundation of writing is interpreting the disorganized thoughts of the writer through language and bringing those ideas to a place of external organization—*coming to terms* with what is initially termless. This is why keeping a journal is often recommended as a form of therapy. However, this only explains the *process* of writing—the easiest and most direct way to *become a writer*—rather than explaining what the goal of a writer should be, something that warrants equal examination.

A good writer is tasked with splitting his veins open with a razor blade and covering his keyboard in blood, a prolonged and terrible ritual. You'll know a piece is finished when your face is numb, eyes unfocused, and body trembling. You'd think Delicious Tacos would have something like this—the horrible reality of being on the writing grind—considering I learned it from reading his work.

The only writer worth reading is an honest writer. How close can he cut things to actual reality? *Actual reality* may seem like hyperbole to those who read garbage, but anyone worth being a member of your audience understands that reality is layered and access to its core takes teeth-gnashing grit. How long can you keep your face in a bee's nest? How long can you last underwater, acknowledging that loneliness and despair are inherent to meaningful progress? You're a fat woman eating ice cream in front of her bathroom mirror. Look away and you lose.

You need to understand yourself. You must come to grips with your genuine intentions, burning away the lies you tell yourself to make it past midnight. Understanding who you really are, unless you're awesome, is going to be fucking awful. Chances are that most of what you know about yourself and your relationships have been total bullshit, fanciful stories and forced narrations which have little relevance to *actual reality*. An honest writer is brutally familiar with the awful person he really is and the meaningless relationships he's forged.

Once you're ready to move beyond the *self*, an honest writer must maintain an accurate understanding of the *outside world*. "You must become a master of human nature," says Robert Greene, and he's right. However, understanding this really sucks; long story short, it's all super uncomfortable. People are massively flawed, entirely selfish, and have very little autonomy; this includes you, but it also includes everyone you've ever loved or respected.

You can now fully diagnose your father's insecurities and trace their root to when your mother began chipping away at his sense of self-worth. You can understand how your mother was toxified by elements that have nothing to do with your family or community and were thought up by people whom you'll never know. You'll understand what your ex-girlfriend really thinks of you, even if you remember your time with her "fondly" and still believe you "had something special." You'll come to know the duplicitous nature of everyone around you. You are the only one in touch with reality and everyone else is to be studied, critiqued, and written about.

Being an honest writer comes in two parts, both of which must be mastered. Self-knowledge and a firm grip on the way things work are non-negotiable; these are items on the *front-end*. They often exist in fragments within the mind of the writer. Writing is about bringing these fragments to proper form through language; the job of the writer is doing this with elegance and beauty.

Writing with authenticity, or writing with a *distinct voice*, is what separates the adequate from the potentially great. Having *good content*—knowing how shit really goes down and blasting your audience with hard doses of heavy truth—is cool and all, but doing it with a form so beautiful that the words sound like they're singing to you when read aloud is breathtaking. An authenticity so earthy and visceral that the truth held within seems tangible and so intimate that it feels as though the writer directed the piece to you personally, a truth you can almost hold in your hands.

✱✱✱

I don't remember her name, but I know that she had herpes. No, that isn't the title of a *Japanese porno*,[12] it's real! It's true! I swear it happened, and it was serendipitous. It was beautiful. Beyond coincidence. As if God knew that I had to interact with this sexually-compromised woman so I could fully tune into the high-frequency signal that Delicious Tacos was quietly broadcasting; real, genuine truth. Total authenticity. *Actual reality.* No bullshit veneer between the reader and his words.

You have this moment when you meet a woman with herpes where you think you've really lucked out. Before the big reveal, of course. Where you think you've found this down-to-Earth girl who could just shoot the shit with you; no games. Where you feel comfortable *being yourself*, yet still feel as though you're respected as a man. Who has the same sexual proclivities as you, who seems to enjoy being humiliated; a shame fetish, I suspected. You think to yourself, *could this be what it means to find a soulmate? Could this have been my "one and only someone?"*

No, stupid, she just has herpes, and much like the burning and irritation it causes her genitals, such is the guilt she feels when she meets someone new.

So, she tells you. She confides in you. You've already built a rapport. She's shown you that she's *different*. She's cool. No pretensions. She thinks it's interesting that you'd get turned on by watching her cry; this is new ground for her. Yes, you could verbally demean her. She's hated herself for so long that it's become a part of her sexual identity. She tells you about her herpes because she thinks she's built up some kind of equity with you.

She tells you that you probably already have it; "most people have it," if you didn't know. And if you (somehow) don't already have it, you definitely won't get it from her; she "hardly ever has an outbreak," and when she does, it's "barely noticeable."

She tells you these things because she can't bear to lie anymore. The countless men she's spread her leprosy to through silence and omission haunt her dreams. So she's cultivated the *perfect girlfriend* personality type. Had she only done so before infection, maybe she'd be married with children, but she won the unlucky lottery and here we are.

The perfect girlfriend. Everything you've ever wanted in a woman, with one little defect, but how about it? You had your mom buy you that pair of Air Jordans in 1992 with the tiny red dot on them that you hoped your sixth grade class would never notice, and that worked out okay, so isn't this the same?

Sorry. Fuck no.

A few days later, I found the Delicious Tacos essay "Girls with Herpes," and it was all there; everything she had said, presciently described by Tacos, written years before I had met her, as if he peered into my future and told my fortune. Tacos was in touch with the kind of reality that typically falls through the cracks and goes unforeseen, the horror that lies between the lines. This was a deeper reach into *actual reality* than I had ever experienced. Tacos wasn't afraid to find these depths and explore them.

Delicious Tacos is more than a dating blogger; he's a modern prophet.

Writing a "fuck blog" is a clever cover for a heady examination of reality, and Delicious Tacos is a master of reality. He's come to terms with himself and his intentions and he's integrated this self-knowledge into the foundational truth of all writing that follows: only sex is real. And since male sexuality has been stigmatized as something inherently evil, the average man will jump through hoops to prove that he's cool, that he's *different*, that he'd be the *perfect boyfriend*, that he's not pathetically horny like everyone else.

How you respond to this will reveal your level of delusion.

Where you stand on the idea of "wanting sex with every female friend and acquaintance you've ever had" has everything to do with how honest you're willing to be. The idea of platonic intergender relationships sounds like a never-ending episode of *Friends* (1994)—just sitting around a coffee shop dishing gossip with your gal-pals, who are dating men more successful, more handsome, and more masculine than you—but that's okay, you're just dying to hear about their big dicks.

No! Bullshit! You lie in wait, carefully biding your time like Montresor in "The Cask of Amontillado" (1846). If you dare say that isn't you, half-crazed, ranting to yourself as she tells you about how her boyfriend *only seems like* an abusive asshole but really has a *sweet sensitive side,* you're a liar, and reading *The Pussy* (2016) will make you feel like an asshole.

HEARTBREAK AND *BIG* (1988)

"Who wants honey? As long as there's some money. Who wants that honey?"

In a flash, Amy was able to transform our heteronormative experience back into something she was more comfortable with, her own safe space of gender neutrality, with the magic words: "get this shit off me." Tossing her the tissue box, I chastised her for *breaking the narrative*, something usually reserved for slightly longer than 15 seconds after sex. Amy may have rolled her eyes, but the fact of the matter remains: sex is the *narrative of attraction.*

Sex is like editing a documentary. Everything is based in reality, but it's up to you to put the story together. Initial attraction may be there, but if you don't string things along the right way, you're not getting laid. Both sexes have their role in building this narrative. It's too easy to reduce the female's role to that of a moviegoer or theater attendee, "just start the damn show and hope I don't walk out." Although there is truth to this dynamic, the woman has her part in showing up *fit for the performance.*

If she's had the bad luck of being out with a doofus, only minimal effort is required. The slightest exertion of feminine prowess will allow her total control of the situation. The aesthetic stakes rise alongside the value of the man interested. By the time she shows up to the date, he'll already know if he wants to fuck her or not—from there, as long as she doesn't commit an egregious, narrative disrupting error of anti-sexuality, her job is mostly done—any further action on her part is for sport.

As a man falls under the aesthetic spell of a woman, he'll construct the rest of the narrative on his own with very little input from her. Did she try to make a joke? It's hilarious! Did she make a super-obvious observation?

She's so smart! Is there any kind of minor nuance to her behavior that can be focused on and doted over? She's adorable! His misguided interpretation of her qualities will remain until his attraction for her has been extinguished, which may be accompanied by feelings of sadness, guilt, shame, or even disgust, depending on the particulars of the situation.

Since anything beyond her aesthetic may be his narrative imposing on reality, there isn't a lingering question of *authenticity*; he wants to believe the lie. Ironically, the authenticity of her beauty is actually debatable—women have an entire arsenal of weapons to deceive the gullible[13]—however, most men are only looking for surface-level approval.

Conversely, authenticity is a central question for her, an ongoing issue to which her attraction to him is contingent upon. She will also see what she wants and lie to herself, but rather than constructing a false narrative based on his aesthetic, she'll magnify the fragments of his personality that she finds attractive and come to the conclusion that he "must always be like that." This is as much a naive fantasy as his personifying her beauty into the idealized girlfriend. While he's putting his *best foot forward* on their date in an attempt to have a sex-worthy performance, she's going along for the ride believing that he's *being himself* and this decisive, assertive, cool, and confident guy is *just who he is*.

Only it isn't so easy; women are savvier in this department than men. She'll subconsciously match his behavior to what he looks like while trying to determine if he *should be* entitled to behavior so decisive, assertive, cool, and confident; any aesthetic less than masculine isn't permitted such attributes[14]. And if this scan turns up negative, she'll think he's faking his swagger and will aggressively test the depth of his authenticity. If he's able to hold it together for long enough, he'll get laid.

All human relationships contain a degree of narrative, requiring effort and social grooming, because we're really just animals on a dirty rock floating through space. But, yes, we have the capacity of forming intimate relationships with one another, and that can be a great experience…or a devastatingly disappointing experience…or something so torturous that it becomes mentally crippling. Even the bonds of family are held together by narrative, and if this seems inaccurate to you, you likely don't know the pain of a distant mother or an absent father.

There is no greater emotional pain than of a narrative dissolving.

Death, of course, is the ultimate narrative dissolution…but short of an ending so dramatic, there is an element of innocence lost for good when a relationship falls into disrepair. When you can take a step back and recognize the true peak, the trust and good feelings that went with it, and even if you're not conscious of the narrative elements that engendered the connection, you're highly aware of your new status as strangers.

If one can crystallize heartbreak to a single moment, it is this intersection between confidant and stranger.

I find this moment to be the most pivotal scene in Penny Marshall's masterpiece *Big* (1988), where the adolescent-in-an-adult-body Josh is with girlfriend Susan at Sea Point Park after having just crossed the metaphorical point of no return, using the magical Zoltar machine to wish away his adult life. After watching *Big* for the first time in years, this scene carried such tremendous emotional weight—which I hadn't remembered, nor prepared for—that I found myself re-watching it so many times consecutively I had to turn the whole thing off and compose myself. This silly 1980's Tom Hanks comedy had hit a raw nerve, unexpectedly, and I needed distance from it.

The moment, perfectly executed, between Hanks and Perkins manages to use the fantasy elements of *Big* as a means to convey an accurate portrayal of the most heartbreaking moment of a break-up; the moment where it's acknowledged that the narrative has been destroyed.

When the normalcy of yesterday becomes the reality of today.

***

We were in her car getting pizza. Kasie's car, because mine was in the shop. Things didn't feel strained as we waited for our order, but the ride home got heavy. After three years, the days blend together and it's easy to get too comfortable. Although it wasn't spoken of explicitly, we knew what was coming, but like a terminally ill patient hoping for *just another day*, we wanted to put off the inevitable…but something happened on the way home. I can't recall exactly what was said, but something triggered a long conversation, with a hot pizza box on my lap, in the passenger seat of her car. And after saying our goodbyes, I tossed the cold pizza in the garbage on the way into my apartment and went to bed.

***

The fantasy element of *Big* allows for a rarely seen big-screen adaptation of the terminally ill breakup scenario, which is usually a bit too low-action for Hollywood, but provides the opportunity for tremendous emotional depth.

Josh and Susan were forced by a power greater than themselves to end their relationship in a manner entirely irrevocable; Josh was living in a world which he was unsuited for; a 13-year-old can only fake his way up the corporate ladder for so long…and while this moment was sad for Josh, he liked dating Susan and screwing Elizabeth Perkins, he wanted to return to his family and his comfortable adolescent life, more likely the better man for his glimpse into adulthood.

But like any story worth telling, the experience of watching *Big* will vary according to the age of the viewer…a child watching *Big* will understand the story as Josh's journey into the esoteric adult world with all adult characters in this journey acting as elaborate props to aid Josh in his experience. With this framework, Susan serves as the *girlfriend accessory* for Josh to have a truly thorough experience. However, an adult watching *Big* will understand the story as equally owned by Susan as a fully-realized character, and by the end of the film may be more in tune with her character arc as Josh walks home in his oversized suit.

While their breakup may have been sad for Josh, it's absolutely devastating for Susan. To appreciate this, it feels important to understand exactly who Susan is. Susan is an unmarried woman in her thirties who begrudgingly works in corporate America, a job which, like Josh, she isn't well-suited for. Susan has had a string of failed relationships with co-workers and is currently involved with a man whom she doesn't particularly seem to like, but it's implied that Susan is drawn to the most successful men at MacMillan Toys…ideals that Susan was raised to believe: become the strong independent woman and date the most successful men. If Susan wasn't raised in Manhattan—something impossible to know—she certainly came to the big city with these goals in mind.

And with these goals in mind, Susan meets Josh, first as an invisible data-entry clerk making less than $200 weekly. No matter how quirky and charming Josh could have been in this capacity, Susan never would have noticed him. It's only when Josh raises his profile at MacMillan, becoming vice president in name only, that Susan takes notice and throws herself at him solely due to his corporate success. But Josh, as a 13-year-old, doesn't *get it*. Josh inadvertently rejects Susan's sexual advances while tapping into something much greater. For Susan, Josh has proven his value by falling backwards into corporate success. But unlike what Susan has become accustomed to with the typical corporate sharks she dates, Josh has an easy presence and an obvious sincerity; Josh is genuine because that's all Josh knows.

Susan falls in love with Josh because he meets her *minimum standard* for a man whom she'd consider dating—career success—while not coming attached with all the baggage that career success will bring: a boring, stressed-out, alcoholic asshole. This was likely something Susan hadn't considered possible as she's gotten older and more jaded, but Josh manages to be so refreshingly different—while also *necessarily the same*—that Susan is able to take the qualities she likes about Josh and impose her own narrative to fill-in the gaps…almost as if aging Susan is intentionally ignoring Josh's childlike behavior, something comically obvious to the audience, in a desperate attempt to hold the whole thing together.[15]

The moment Susan acknowledges the impossible, that Josh is actually a 13-year-old body-switched into an adult, the *point of no return* for a breakup has been crossed, and in this case, it feels like a strange combination of Josh's death and the idea that Josh never actually existed.[16]

When Susan reaches out to hug Josh one last time—the kind of hug where you don't want to let go—it serves as the transition point between the romanticized yesterday and the coldness of today. Susan realizes that Josh only existed as her narrative, that she magnified the fragments of his personality which she found attractive while willfully ignoring what she didn't want to see…but the strength of reality intervened, destroying her narrative entirely. And *Big* feels like Susan's story when she laments how Josh won't remember her, revealing the sad truth of the matter. While Josh's experience with Susan was significant, it wasn't significant in the same way that it was to Susan.

Like a child watching *Big*, Susan existed as an accessory for Josh, the gateway into a different world; the esoteric experiences of adulthood. For Susan, the narrative of Josh represented relief and salvation from that very same world, a world which couldn't deliver on the promises it made to a younger, more innocent Susan. For Susan, Josh felt like her last chance to make good.

AUTHENTICITY AND *THE CABLE GUY* (1996)

"I'd rather be anywhere, doing anything..."

There was a gleam in her eye when *Ghostbusters* (2016) came up in the group's discussion. She corrected the speaker, a male, who didn't make an elaborate point to reference the movie's notorious gender component; "the new *Ghostbusters*," he offhandedly called it, but this was "girl *Ghostbusters*," she said with pride. After all, she was a high school science teacher and this was a victory with which she could attach herself.

This attachment was the point, existing independently of the movie. She may not see it, nor should she have to; her attachment to "girl *Ghostbusters*" had served to bolster her identity. The actual film is an afterthought, a big budget talking point. Beyond all the fuss, *Ghostbusters* is a pile of crap with regurgitated jokes, so who really cares?

The modern addiction is identity. The impulse to create a large inventory of bullet points which can be used to detail an image of unique superiority. A strong and intelligent woman should like a movie about female vigilante scientists, that's easy; a real no-brainer, and then it's on to the next talking point in a neverending continuum. And that's why "girl *Ghostbusters*" will be dead in the water by the time it hits theaters; the audience has already cannibalized it and moved on.

All identities are not created equally. The game isn't about mutual acceptance, the game is about *superiority,* and when the stakes are high, there must be standards; judgment necessitates regulation. As the race toward becoming the smartest and most unique grows increasingly rigorous, so does our sensitivity toward the potential inauthenticity of the identity being crafted.

I went to a foodie kind of restaurant with a date. Date knew the chef. Afterwards, the chef asked what our least favorite dish was. I was unaware, at the time, that this was a loaded question not meant to be answered. I told him I didn't love the dark chocolate liver pate. Everyone around me got nervous. I got nervous. I said maybe it was just me. They agreed.

I didn't understand, at the time, that this was more than just a meal at a restaurant—an enjoyable intermission between one activity and the next—but, rather, I was an attendant to an experience. My reaction to this experience said a lot about my depth of sophistication. The chef was testing the authenticity of that depth; was I *really* one of them? My answer suggested that I wasn't. My date got nervous; I had potentially embarrassed her. The vibe became uncomfortable, and I recovered by outing myself as a tourist in an unfamiliar world; having a least favorite dish was *my own issue*, an issue hopefully born out of inexperience and not a lack of sophistication entirely, a mortal sin in this landscape.

Authenticity testing is the natural consequence to "identity as accessory" becoming part of the mainstream consciousness. To understand this shift, we can look to *Fight Club* (1999), when Edward Norton explains that he seeks to express self-definition through his consumer habits, asking "What kind of dining set defines me as a person?" Rather than starting at self-knowledge and moving forward, like Norton would have you believe, he's instead thinking about how *he'd like to* define himself as a person; the assumption he casually makes is that the authenticity of these choices is inherent. This observation would no longer seem clever for a modern audience; we understand that our choices serve to define who we *want to be* rather than expressing who we are, and this has created a paranoid pop culture where authenticity is always suspect.

There is a decadence to this obsession with authenticity. Our culture fosters a kind of Holden Caulfield-like suspended adolescence where wearing the Metallica shirt isn't enough, nor is it immediately permissible, but only after an undefined quantity of experience is your ownership of the shirt acceptable. Are you sophisticated enough to understand *why you should* enjoy dark chocolate liver pate, regardless of personal taste? Are you watching *Mrs. Doubtfire* (1993) the right way, ironically and detached, or following the film's narrative as intended?[17]

If the obsession with authenticity is a luxury, indicative of a culture so problem-free that it's boring itself to death, to what degree is any expectation of authenticity reasonable?

Like Edward Norton in *Fight Club,* Jim Carrey's lonely, television-obsessed cable guy in *The Cable Guy* (1996) is never given a proper name, and like in *Fight Club,* this is to imply that Carrey is both everyman and no-man simultaneously, a cultural composite and a blank slate. Carrey is useful to Matthew Broderick's character of Steven Kovacs, an average joe doofus, throughout the course of the film; initially as an underhanded cable installer ready to work his magic and give Kovacs free cable—something of a 1990's urban legend—and later as a crucial element in Kovacs' ailing relationship. Throughout the film, their motivations are always clear: the cable guy wants Kovacs' friendship and Kovacs wants to get rid of the cable guy despite begrudgingly enjoying the cable guy's quirky offerings.

Kovacs immediately recognizes the cable guy's usefulness beyond free cable; when the cable guy tells him to "thirst for knowledge" of his ex-girlfriend's "complicated spender," Kovacs finds it "incredibly insightful" and implements it the following day, even after learning that it came from an episode of *The Jerry Springer Show* (1991). The cable guy suggests Kovacs invite her over for dinner, *Sleepless in Seattle* (1993) was showing on HBO; Steven follows along here, too, and is met with a surprisingly positive reception from Robin, the frigid ex.

Although grossly overused, there is something to a woman's accusation of a man being a "creeper." Follow around a beautiful woman and you'll see awkward men fumble about while attempting contrived small talk, or so I've heard. Say what you will about female privilege in the Western world, but this shit is fucking uncomfortable. These men stand out because their interactions are so boldly unnatural and *inauthentic* that their agenda is entirely evident; it isn't about connecting with the woman at all, and even if she's just an attractive sexual vessel for the more nondescript men she interacts with, they are able to hide their intentions and seem authentic, while the creeper fails in this regard and stands out as "icky."

Humans are wired with a social radar that rejects awkward or unnatural behavior that makes us uncomfortable. We require that our interactions seem natural. The audience is presented with Carrey as a social creeper; the cable guy is anything but natural. When he crashes Steven's pickup basketball game, his desire to be included seems too *preplanned* for pickup basketball, which is meant to be spontaneous. This is like how the girl at the bar going home with the pickup artist doesn't want to believe their interaction was set up by a man looking for sex; she wants to think it was something special that *just happened.*

When the cable guy is included in the game, his social inadequacies become glaring. If we dissect Carrey's thought process here, it seems logically sound: the guys are playing basketball, so he shows up in what he considers serious athletic gear, he plays harder than everyone— misunderstanding the term *friendly competition*—and since Kovacs is his target for friendship, he demands to be on Steven's team. To someone who doesn't understand the natural dance of socialization, this would seem like how you'd ingratiate yourself into a new group: by proving your value and loyalty. When the cable guy shatters the backboard on a slam dunk, a scene straight out of the climax of a movie, he expects to be met with high-fives…but, of course, that isn't how real life works. Embarrassed, Steven makes it clear that the two aren't friends.

Until the next scene, when Steven's television service is disrupted. Without *Sleepless in Seattle,* he seems lost with Robin, so he's happy to use his friend the cable guy to fix things. Throughout the rest of the film, Steven's and Robin's relationship only progresses with Carrey's intervention, which begs the question: what do they really have in common? If a hollow sound bite from *Jerry Springer* is enough to mend things, what does it say about the relationship's authenticity?

And suddenly it seems as though Steven is the inauthentic social creeper when compared to the awkward and lonely cable guy. While Steven knows what to say and how to act in order to fit in socially, he lacks true depth, which speaks to his inability to maintain Robin's interest on his own. The cable guy may be inauthentic on the surface, but he displays a raw emotion that the viewer can relate to.

A comedy is considered dark when it cuts too close to reality. The characters in a dark comedy are more complex; there is often a sadness beyond the laughter. A dark comedy can produce feelings of guilt! what does it say about us if we find Jim Carrey's portrayal of *lonely desperation* funny? And, what might be more troubling, how much of the cable guy do we see in ourselves?

How you view the scene at Medieval Times may answer this question. Are you like Steven and find Medieval Times inherently embarrassing, or would you be able to lose yourself in the moment and have a good time? And, if not, what would you think of the people around you who were there to have fun? In the war of identity superiority, our greatest weapon is judgment.

So what did we learn about authenticity? Get good at being cool, and people will like you; act socially retarded, and you'll be treated like a buffoon.

Oh, and always remember to like the dark chocolate liver pate.

UNDERACHIEVERS

"I wanna publish 'zines and rage against machines..."

Toward the end of 1990, you couldn't get away from *Simpsons* merchandise—from posters, to pajama sets, to pencil toppers—mostly featuring Generation X's very first mainstream media icon, Bart Simpson. You see, before *The Simpsons* (1989) became fixated on Homer's gradual decline into retardation, the show's initial protagonist was skateboarding prankster Bart, the country's first take on their next generation.

And those savvy *Simpsons* writers seemed to have nailed it. While Bart's driving characteristic was apathy, it was a kind of *self-aware* apathy. Bart wasn't stupid, he was an "underachiever"; he was capable of more, but consciously chose less. This hyper-aware apathy would become the generation's defining trait. The following year, Kurt Cobain was hailed as the "voice of Generation X," releasing Nirvana's seminal *Nevermind* (1991) record. The standout single, "Smells Like Teen Spirit," served to define the generation with the very same self-conscious apathy: "I feel stupid and contagious; here we are now, entertain us."

Generation X was most proud of their ability to know they were disappointing. Not only did they believe this understanding negated the negative implications of being so disappointing—if you know you're a loser, you're not really a loser—but it was also the foundation of their identity. Generation X was too cool for their own good.

And even if that line in "Teen Spirit" seemed to sum up the zeitgeist of the generation quite nicely, it turned out Cobain wasn't actually their spokesman after all. You wouldn't know it if you didn't live through it, but Nirvana took on a mythology after Cobain's suicide in the middle of

1994. This was understandable; as grim as it may be, is there anything more authentic than suicide? And authenticity was the holy grail for the detail-obsessed, Holden Caulfield-like GenXer; Cobain offing himself put Nirvana miles ahead of their peers and gave their music an added dimension of reality. But the truth is that Nirvana had already begun to fall apart in the months leading to the suicide. Their third studio album, *In Utero* (1993), was met with a disappointing reception, partially by design. Cobain had become obsessed with the type of person who would buy a Nirvana record. Never before had *audience* been a consideration for a rock star, who typically only cares about pushing enough records to sell out suburban hockey arenas. No one stops to consider who's actually *buying the records* because who fucking cares?

This type of anxiety was unique to Generation X; success wasn't enough, it had to be the right kind of success, just as unconscious apathy may be losery, but self-aware apathy takes on a sheen of hip irony. Since Cobain wasn't selling records to the right kind of Nirvana fan—something he had already cried about in the liner notes to *Incesticide* (1992)—Cobain would consciously write a difficult, off-putting record with vocals infamously "low in the mix" in order to whittle the band's audience down to a personality type that Cobain was more comfortable with.

Maybe Cobain earned Nirvana's place in the rock and roll pantheon by sheer will; he was authentically obsessed with authenticity. It was around this time that old man Axl Rose tried to compete with this edgy—albeit neurotic—conception of cool by performing a Charles Manson song on his band's rather terrible cover album, *The Spaghetti Incident?* (1993). Poor Boomer Axl was out of his depth, although it's tough to compete with someone who has nothing to lose…as if you'd want to. Kurt Cobain was too cool for his own good.

***

Green Day will go down as the historically less regarded alternative rock Cinderella story. Emerging from the shadow of Cobain's suicide, Green Day shot to stardom over the summer of 1994 and by the end of the year were selling out their own suburban hockey arenas. So popular were the Berkeley trio that they singlehandedly resurrected punk rock, transformed it into something commercially viable, and gave an entire generation of misfit teenagers their first job at Hot Topic. Even old Johnny

Rotten owes a debt to Green Day; in the wake of punk rock's anything-but-chaotic return, the Sex Pistols cashed in on a glitzy, establishment-approved, MTV-promoted reunion tour. God save the Queen indeed, only this time they really meant it.

Green Day had a lot in common with Nirvana. Both were fascinated with nihilism, melancholy, and angst- a hallmark of the generation. However, unlike Cobain, who felt a sense of betrayal when confronting what he considered the meaninglessness of modernity, Green Day reveled in disaster. Imagining them both as teenagers at a house party, Nirvana is sulking alone, smoking cigarettes, and Green Day is taking hits of canned air and giggling. So suicide wasn't in the cards, an idea that must have thrilled their record label. However, it wasn't all giggles and huffing; despite signing a corporate record deal, filming music videos for MTV, and booking an arena tour—surprise, surprise—like Cobain, Green Day suddenly had a problem with the kind of person buying Green Day records. On their first arena tour, to punish the presumed jocks and frat boys in attendance, the band booked an aggressively homosexual "queercore" group in the form of Pansy Division to open for them and taunt the audience with songs like "The Butt Fuckers of Rock and Roll," and "Smells Like Queer Spirit."

Like the bratty teenager who didn't get the right kind of Corvette for their *Super Sweet Sixteen* (2007), despite their quick and easy ascendance to the top of the alt-rock mountain, it wasn't the *right kind of success*. And just like Nirvana, Green Day penned their very own audience-shedding record. Released a year after *Dookie* (1994), *Insomniac* (1995) did its job rather well; it was good but not great, didn't have a hit single, and ultimately turned their audience against them.[18,19]

Despite all the nihilistic posturing, it's important to remember that Generation X wasn't the one with all the school shootings. The murky attitude was as shallow as the cuts on their wrists; it was a fashion accessory, it was an act, it was total bullshit. Even if they didn't become noteworthy go-getters, GenX eventually had to grow up into lame adults. A few years after Green Day did everything they could to torture their audience, they had a song featured on the finale of *Seinfeld* (1998), which was viewed by over 70 million people. If selling out is inevitable, you may as well cut the best deal you can and get on with it. Just like GenX, Green

Day were growing up into lame adults; turns out they weren't very cool after all.

Green Day continued to be the voice of their generation as they all hurdled toward taking center stage as the world's grownups. When Generation X thought making fun of Fox News was the height of *woke political awareness,* Green Day released *American Idiot* (2004). GenX was still bent on thinking they were the coolest people in the room, only now with a new definition of cool to keep up with.

Generation-X became the first generation to treat *identity* as a consumer product, to be carefully considered, procured and groomed. Whether they wanted to be perceived as self-aware ironic losers or *woke political analysts,* thinking they were the right kind of cool was a chief priority. And if aging GenX wanted to see a gaudy Broadway musical, as lame adults inevitably do, Green Day was there for them again: *American Idiot* (2010) was transformed into a Broadway show for the GenXer who thought they were too cool for *Guys and Dolls* (2009).

There will never be a GenX president. They weren't a generation interested in changing the world; as long as they have the right emoji reaction to this week's tragedy on their Facebook profile, that's good enough for them. Generation X is neither the hero nor the villain of the story—they didn't do as much damage as their big brothers the Boomers, nor are they on the front line of the culture war like their sisters the millennials—and besides, they're much too cool for all of that, anyway.

DEFIANCE ON THE ROAD TO DECAY

"I'm not dead, I'm not for sale..."

The waning days of August. After midnight; 2AM about to roll around as inconspicuously as the 80,000[th] mile on the odometer of an old girl who won't quit. *Not quite ready to bring it down just yet.*[20] Miles of quiet. Last man standing. Watching the tide roll in. Everything leading to this feels weighted and opaque, a dull ache only noticeable in moments of stillness. When you're young, there's a timelessness to the hours before dawn. They dissipate in the moonlight. The keys to your dad's old beater will open up the world around you like never before, possibilities expanding beyond the infinite. Everything with a veneer of significance. Sitting at a diner and only ordering coffee. Telling ghost stories on old country roads. Hopping fences and trashing swimming pools. Searchlights in graveyards on Saturday nights.

Once this is lost, it's gone for good. You get to an age where late nights just feel late. But you search for little bits and pieces of it. Maybe you drink to forget that the clock is always watching; a grim, invasive specter. If you have anything left to give—any mark left to make—you're coming up on *now or never*. This is something an adult can never forget, no matter how many drinks he's had.

But on the beach at 2AM, I can dip my toes into the realm of the timeless. Close my eyes and for a scant moment feel at one with the world around me. If you've never felt it, even if just for a moment, you'll think I'm selling you on some bullshit, but it's true and it's beautiful. And it's only for a scant moment until I'm reminded of why I'm at the beach so late as electricity pulses down my spine and my legs anxiously fumble about the sand.

I'm at the beach at 2AM because I've been awake for the past 48 hours.

***

If masculinity is power,[21] there is a defiance inherent to masculinity. The masculine man lives on his own terms, resisting the world's inertia insisting he conform. He assesses risk and reward and takes pride in making his own decisions. No better a glimpse of defiant masculinity than the combat sports fighter. He understands the game, he evaluates the risk, and he visualizes the reward. Even the losing fighter garners the respect of participation—the only participation trophy that matters—and walks away with a warrior's honor and the gorgeous women who find that irresistible.

The feminized world cannot come to grips with the defiance of masculinity. It misunderstands the high-risk/high-reward dichotomy, foolishly believing that the participants are *unaware* of the risks or else they wouldn't hunt for rewards. The feminized worldview is steeped in consumerism—the proverbial activity punch card at summer camp, the bucket-list life—where the longer life is understood as the better life. If not for a long life, how else can one enjoy food, wine, and travel?

The modern male exists as an infection of consumerism. To the male consumer, there is no higher degree of satisfaction than money and women-;not wicked in their own right, but neither should be ends in themselves. The masculine man will demand a deeper experience, spitting in the face of risk to attain something which transcends what the consumer can understand. When a man's goal is money and women, they'll settle for achieving either with the least amount of energy exerted, leaving them enslaved to a master both at home and at work.

When Robert Frost wrote "A Time to Talk,"[22] a reminder that there is more to life than working, the perspective was masculine. It is the masculine inclination to use time productively, not to consume but to *produce,* so much that Frost felt as though a reminder was needed that there is value in moments of rest, that a man entirely consumed with productivity is a man living in isolation. There must exist a time to work and a *time to talk;* empty spaces in life, spaces without immediate utility. The feminized man, as infected by consumerism, does not understand life this way; always looking to minimize effort and maximize pleasure, the feminized man cannot stop talking.

Making *time to talk* is critical for the masculine man, a necessary reminder that productivity can be an abyss.

✳✳✳

I'll have this moment when a coworker asks what I did over the summer and inevitably tells me of some weeklong cruise or family trip to Wally World, where I think of loperamide hydrochloride. If you didn't know, loperamide hydrochloride is more commonly sold as Imodium AD, an over-the-counter diarrhea remedy. And I have this moment where I think of 3AM, lying in bed, desperately reading about the dangers of taking loperamide hydrochloride to treat opiate withdrawal.

It's a funny story, I swear.

When a man transcends the feminine, summer camp, bucket-list life and becomes attune to looking at his time on Earth as the maximization of productivity—pure creative output, total content mindset—he inevitably begins looking for ways to squeeze the most blood from a stone. How can I sleep best, when it's time to sleep, and work hardest when it's time to work, risks be damned. It was toward the waning days of spring when I discovered kratom.[23]

What the anti-drug crowd never mentions is the difference between drug use and drug abuse. Conceptually, these are separate and distinct, however difficult it may be for the drug user to avoid abuse. The masculine man, captain of his own ship, can assess the risks and visualize the rewards. There are upsides to drug use for the masculine man, looking beyond the depth of consumption, to maximize productivity. There's a reason writers are alcoholics and opiate and cocaine addicts: *because it works*. Snort a few lines and open up your word processor—get into a flow state, feel your presence, laugh like a maniac at your own jokes, enrich your mind-body connection—pure creative output, total content mindset. The masculine drug user isn't looking to masturbate his emotions with an artificial light show; the masculine drug user is obsessed with squeezing blood from a stone.

✳✳✳

Arguably the best Stone Temple Pilots album is *Purple* (1994). Maligned for being a few months late to the grunge party, and maybe edging too close to parody with their debut, *Purple* redefined STP's sound by replacing the darker, grungy riffs with trippy, psychedelic rock. More was possible with this lighter, experimental version of the band; gone was the joyless sludge of "Dead and Bloated," replaced by the radio-friendly "Interstate Love Song." Gone was the histrionic "Wet My Bed," replaced by the understated "Big Empty." The Pilots no longer had to explicitly sell you on their dark intentions; they would allow the music to convey it organically, as with the subtly haunting "Kitchenware and Candybars."

The cover art to *Purple*—a smiling baby riding a dragon while a group of angelic women look on with wonder—was found printed on the first bag of heroin Scott Weiland ever bought. In fact, a lot of *Purple* is about Weiland's heroin use, which began on their first tour; "Unglued" details the manic height of defiant experimentation while "Vasoline" laments the sobering reality of addiction.

According to his own account, Purple was recorded "outside of time and space." With heroin, Weiland was able to tap into the timeless space of youth, a place of pure creativity. Maximum possibilities; pushing things beyond the infinite.[24]

***

Finding my sweet spot with kratom took a bit of clumsy trial and error. The powder tastes awful, so the flavor needs to be masked. I fell into a groove of taking it toward the late afternoon into early evening; this quickly became, very precisely, 5:15 PM. I would time my after-work gym session to finish around 5PM so I could be home by 5:15, mix my 15 grams of kratom with almond milk and flavored protein powder (a bolder flavor, like chocolate malt or rocky road worked best), and get to work. Kratom was fantastic for productivity. I'd sit down to write and let the words take on a life of their own—outside of time and space—pure creative output, total content mindset. I was happier on kratom and more social. Soon I was taking kratom before seeing friends and meeting women. I was better with girls on kratom; I felt one with body and mind. *Moderation is masturbation;* I went from "once in a while" to every other day to every day. As addictive as Tylenol and as safe as coffee. I had found a way to squeeze blood from a stone.

***

A concrete, static timeline is inherent to drug use; heroin is not known for its generosity. After producing a fantastic third album with Stone Temple Pilots, Weiland had hit his creative peak and came tumbling down. Within months of releasing the wonderfully bizarre *Tiny Music...Songs from the Vatican Gift Shop* (1996), the Pilots had to cancel their supporting tour, pulling out of a coveted opening spot for the KISS reunion, and would soon disband entirely. Weiland had traded long-term stability for short-term creative mania, like finding the invincibility star in *Super Mario Bros.* (1985), and was saddled with a debt to repay.

I began feeling awful so gradually that it wasn't immediately noticeable; it felt more like a new normal. Kratom isn't heroin. The decline isn't sharp; it's subtle. I noticed that I was losing my trademark, high-energy morning enthusiasm; getting to work was becoming a drag. A symptom of getting older, I had assumed. I was becoming more irritable, more prone to frustration, more prone to insomnia, more prone to constipation. My legs began to ache constantly; was my leg day that strenuous? I found myself counting down the hours until 5:15 PM...and when summer rolled around, I figured that I'd dose earlier and then hit a second batch later that night.

Double the dose, double the productivity. Total content...something or other? Actually, I was posting on Twitter more than I was doing any real writing; I wanted that hard, immediate dopamine hit. I was distracted and aimless. I had gotten what I could from kratom and it was time for a break. No problem, I had thought—a few weeks off to clean-up and recharge—then I could get back on and get back to work.

***

Pacing my tiny kitchen at 10PM—heart racing, legs aching—dealing with a downward spiral of denial that was overwhelming. The worst case, I had assumed, was some kind of psychological attachment—addiction for the weak—something I could push through with sheer will. I had quit smoking earlier in the year, and yes, I had spent the week compensating with pizza and ice cream, but I took care of the fucker. Will and determination; I could push through anything. But I was never expecting a *physical dependency*.

Kratom came with a debt to be paid.

Turns out kratom is highly addictive; funny, right? It's not a supplement, it's a drug. It may come on slowly, but it ends up mimicking genuine opiates; *opiate-like,* indeed. It was the beginning of July and it suddenly became clear exactly how I would be spending my summer vacation.[25]

✳✳✳

Scott Weiland would fall between relapse and recovery for the rest of his life. His work would never again reach the height of the mid-90's. Each relapse took a little more from Weiland, chipping away at him so gradually that it was hardly noticeable at first. He would reunite with the Pilots only to be fired a few years later; he began losing his voice and wasn't able to get through an entire show. Compensating for his failing body, Weiland doubled-down on his drug use, but what had worked in the past to push him to his spiritual limits had only served to destroy what was left. Weiland died a shell of himself, a walking corpse; he had pushed things as far as they could go, he had run out of content, he passed on with nothing left to give.

The moral of the story is that there is no moral. Sorry, Charlie Rose; real life doesn't work that way. 2,000 words later and I don't have some grand conclusion or massive realization. Know the rules of the game and decide how you want to play: a long life of potential mediocrity or a creative energy that burns with the fire of 1,000 suns. The defiant man can make this decision for himself and deal with the consequences of his actions. Dip your toes in the water of creative mania and maybe you can get out alive; fully immerse yourself and watch it kill you.

GRADUATING COLLEGE AND "IN THE BEDROOM" (2002)

"Hung down with the freaks and the ghouls..."

It was my last semester in college, and I wanted to retake "Intro to Creative Writing" because I had gotten a C- in it the first time around and I couldn't allow that on my *permanent record*. It's hard to imagine caring about such things in retrospect, but in the early oughts, I had it in mind to go all the way to my English PhD, and what kind of *doctor of literature* would have gotten a C- in fucking *Intro to Creative Writing*—where the girls write about boys they're fucking who don't want to date them and the boys write about girls they like from afar—who are sometimes sitting in the very same class.

It was in this very same class that I met Kasie, who had written very adorable stories about her boyfriend not calling her on Easter and an entire five pages as a thinly veiled excuse to complain about one of her girlfriends; *whom I knew*, even if Kasie had changed her name to something innocuous, she included enough catty details that made it obvious. I leaned over to her desk and said, "I know who this is..." and watched her turn beet red—a bold move, unwittingly played to great effect—our *meet-cute*.

I wanted "In the Bedroom" (2002) to be the opening of a long and ambitious, post-modernist, suburban fantasy novel; think Pynchon meets Ellis meets *Final Fantasy II* (1991). Where the story would begin as something very narrow and contained—single character, lost in thought, in a small room with a few friends watching television—and somehow end up large and sprawling, encompassing the entire world and beyond, all while maintaining the minimalism of Ellis and the close attention to language that's a trademark of Pynchon.

The piece focused on growing up—the place in-between adolescence and adulthood—where people become who they are and relationships change. This was my world at the time. The irony to the protagonist's refusal to let go was that it mirrored my own, and while writing this, in 2002, I had no idea how difficult the next decade of my life would become—heartbreak, depression—it would be ten years before I didn't feel metaphorically confined to my own bedroom.

In the Bedroom

Ten[26] looked at the table with an almost lively gleam,[27] and after taking a second or so to thoroughly inspect the situation, he blurted out the word "Zenith." With a slight sense of apathy, I slid a synthetic colored tablet under my tongue. Ten took the appropriate amount of off-white Scrabble pieces scattered on top of the muggy bridge table and formed the word. Kristen looked at the new formation suspiciously, like a curious puppy. After seconds, or even minutes, of inspecting and re-inspecting, she exclaimed, "That's not a word, Ten," with the enthusiasm of uncovering a fantastic mystery. Ten fired back, "It is so! Zenith. Triple fucking word score."

"Well, use it in a sentence."

"Zenith...another word for God."

The television buzzed with darkness.

With that, Ten ended the argument. Kristen was satisfied. It was July. It was humid enough to be July, at least. Even in Kat's bedroom, I could feel it blanketing me. My first summer vacation from college was about to end, spent with the people I grew up with. While physically the same, their roles had transformed. Kat was my dealer, Drew joined a band and changed his name to Ten, and Kristen became his pet. Time bound us together. It felt awkward but seemed right. The tablet fizzled under my tongue.

Kat's room smelled like dirt. The crickets were so loud that I wondered if there were a few under her bed. We always seemed to be waiting. Last week, it was for Kitty's music video. Last month, we waited for the *Real World* (1992) marathon, and tonight ,we're sitting anxiously for the new Pepsi commercial.

The spot stars Kitty America, America's latest trademarked pop star. Kitty was electronically rendered by some of the top computer engineers across the country. She could change with the times, but she couldn't grow old. She couldn't get sick and she couldn't run away. She could be a logo forever. Kat and Kristen envied her beauty, and Ten was surely in love. The room tilted and swayed. Under my feet sat the broken-up Scrabble board Ten had destroyed weeks ago.[28] For a moment, I contemplated researching the validity of his "triple word score," but I let it pass. The bridge table was littered with different words created by scrabble pieces, most of which involved or stood for products available at Walmart.

Kat lied motionless on the couch behind us. She wasn't saying much, but she never really did. The walls of her room were decorated with different posters and pin-ups of MTV stars. Her most prized artifact was on the wall directly behind her couch, a poster for the film that christened Hollywood's exploitation of eastern religions, *Dude, Where's My Moksha?* Soon after, Hinduism was everywhere. Bands wrote songs about it; families celebrated its holy days. Cartoonish-looking deity novelties were sold back-to-back with Santa accessories. Kat treated the film as if it were enlightenment itself. The television buzzed, at which Kristen and Ten stared blankly.

A surge came over the group. Immediately it was certain that this was what we were waiting for. The television flickered distinctively. With reborn awareness, we watched the screen as it led us, all in the room together singing: "bada, ba ba ba—bada, ba ba ba." As one, Kristen, Ten, and I all said the words along with Kitty: "the joy of cola." Our attention suddenly turned to Kat, as she was motioning to speak. Words began to curl off her lips: "The Freshmaker." We laughed.[29]

I went along with the others; I said the words. It didn't have the same effect on me as it did on them. There was no reassurance or euphoria. I felt no connection with the television, or Kitty's lips and eyes. The lights danced. The only thing clear was the door to the room, its knob, and me. Ace Frehley's solo to a KISS song I didn't remember pulsated and shot straight through my head. On a rocket ride.

The top was down, the air was cool, and the highway was empty. In the middle of August, dusk begins so late. We would drive around the East End for hours and end up parking right up on the water. Kristen would play with the radio. We sat on the hood of my car and threw rocks into the Sound. When our eyes met, it would feel like the night could never end. We wondered where the purple sand came from. We wondered how sand always got in food at the beach. We spoke about the future as if we could write it. She tugged and tugged the sleeve of my sweatshirt until I was close enough. She kissed me. We could feel the wind, we could feel the night. We slept in my car.

There was just me now. Kat was asleep on the couch. Ten and Kristen were fucking while Kristen kept her eyes fixed on Ten and Ten watched MTV. A video from a band called the Unnecessaries glared off the set. Their song was loud and obliterating. Ten followed every motion lead from the screen. I felt dizzy and sick.

There were three motions separating me from the outside of the room. Probably hundreds of individual movements just getting to the door. I wasn't sure what it mattered, anyway. The street would be dark and I would be alone. It could be filled with people. I would see their faces. They could reach out to me, for me.

Everything blurred and colors ran together, iridescent. Kat's room, my future, Ten's motions, and Kristen. Sometimes things change before you even notice. My head hit the floor. I could feel Kat's fluorescent white lights as they blended into buzzing darkness.

STONED AT WALMART AND "BEING JOHNNY TANGLE" (2006)

"I know you better than you fake it..."

A few years after graduating college, with the idea in mind to become a literature professor, I found myself going to graduate school for a degree to teach high school English. Not a terrible idea entirely, but I was entirely unaware of what made it terrible; I was expecting it to be something that it never was—*genuine*—and this slight in understanding would set me back years.

At the time, I really liked getting stoned and going to Walmart, in a way where, if I let my mind wander, I have fond memories of it like people will of having lived in foreign countries; experiences and exploration. It was as surreal as it was comforting; candy and DVDs, total immersion into the core of consumer culture while dealing with the horror that maybe I was enjoying it just as much as everyone else. Like when people say they *don't like fast food;* you're a liar if part of you doesn't get off on the cheap thrill, even if the relationship is *complicated*.

"Being Johnny Tangle" (2006) was born from this complicated relationship with nostalgia and consumer culture and is the spiritual prequel to "In the Bedroom."

Being Johnny Tangle

"But Mom, seriously, you promised," cried a bewildered Johnny Tangle. Mrs. Tangle gazed into her web of string beans, "Not tonight, Johnny, you know better…tonight is string beans and meatloaf night. It's *been* string beans and meatloaf night for weeks now! You should know this, Johnny, really…and when did I ever promise McDonald's?"

His mother's words shot through Johnny like a spear impaling a lightning bolt. When did she promise McDonald's? He was sure she did, as Dally provided a callous glance from his muted television and MTV. But maybe, possibly, could Johnny Tangle, in a fit of deranged hunger, have imagined that his loving mother of eight (mostly) wonderful years had promised to buy him three Happy Meals?

Three Happy Meals were an absolute necessity in this situation, as McDonald's had begun giving away Hot Wheels in their Happy Meal combination, and there were three variations of the miniaturized model car. Johnny knew there would be three different paint schemes, three different sets of tiny plastic tires, and three different character decals on the hood. How could little Johnny Tangle be expected to choose between Ronald McDonald, Grimace, and the eccentric Hamburglar? It was a choice Johnny knew he wasn't prepared to make.

And then there was the food, the glorious food. Since the first time his mother took him to McDonald's, over the summer for a birthday party, Johnny had craved Ronald's unique blend of sugar and fat. Johnny sat close to Dally, watching his muted television with earmuff headphones on and a cord extending all the way to his room down the hall. Dally would sit watching MTV with the sound turned down for as long as he could while listening to records playing in his bedroom.

"You know, Dally, your father is gonna break his neck one of these days on this freakin' cord," Mrs. Tangle said mostly to herself. She knew Dally couldn't hear her and Johnny only cared about McDonald's. She returned, defeated, to her string beans.

Dally started collecting dust, as Mrs. Tangle put it, when he asked for, and received, his earmuff headphone cord extension set for Christmas. With this special item, Dally would be able to sit in front of the television while listening to his record player running down the hall. He rarely moved, and if you watched closely, he rarely blinked. Johnny never understood why Dally wanted such a boring gift, as Christmas was a time for action figures and mystery goo, and when he asked his father, Mr. Tangle offered: "Son, when you grow up, you'll find that a lot of guys want cord extensions." Mr. Tangle's explanation, which may have been the result of too many rum-zingers, didn't serve to clear up Johnny's bewilderment.

And bewilderment was an emotion that Johnny was becoming too familiar with on that unusually cold September evening. Johnny scanned the television for the time, finding only flashing lights and blinking colors. "We have to act fast, Dally," Johnny said anxiously, "Mom is almost done with the meatloaf! And then I'm going to have to set the table. And I don't wanna set the table for meatloaf, which should really be called grossloaf, and I don't want grossloaf." Dally seemed unfazed, even by his brother's accusation of the night's meal being "gross."

"Someone is calling my hard work gross," Mrs. Tangle said hotly. Johnny peered into the kitchen, as his mother slumped down in Mr. Tangle's seat at the head of the table with her head in her hands. Johnny watched as she sat in silence and plotted his next move. He considered a casual suggestion, to the effect of something like, "Say, I wonder if McDonald's would be any good tonight," or maybe more along the lines of, "I wonder what's going on at McDonald's?" Johnny figured a question would warrant an answer, and the only way to answer such a question would be to pick up and go to McDonald's. Before he could make his move, the door slammed and Mr. Tangle entered the kitchen, sweaty and smelling like Old Spice.

"Meatloaf tonight," Mr. Tangle said with defeat, "gross." Mrs. Tangle's head sank further into her hands, "…You could always come home and make dinner if you don't like my cooking." Mr. Tangle laughed, and Johnny wondered if he didn't get the joke. Now was his chance, and he knew it. He began by straining for indifference, "Guys…we all know the meatloaf's gross, so why don't we go to…" Johnny stopped as his mother's face began turning red. The room fell silent. Johnny could almost hear the solo to a KISS song he didn't know pumping through his brother's earmuff headset.

"Go to your goddamn room, Johnny Tangle. Go to your room and stay there!"

Johnny couldn't help but wonder what he had done wrong. His own father had even agreed that the grossloaf was really, really gross! Johnny kicked the door to his room closed. Behind the door was his brother's old KISS poster, which Johnny never took down when he changed rooms on account of how neat the guys looked in their superhero costumes and makeup.

His eyes fixed on the bunch of "old junk" (Mrs. Tangle's words) that Dally had left in Johnny's new closet. As he gazed, Johnny felt his vision come in and out of focus. What a bunch of junk Dally left behind; the closet was filled with outdated toys, partially-completed crossword puzzles, and the golden arches. Johnny repeated the last part to himself again, this time slowly: "...and the golden arches." What were those beautiful, yellow, curvy arches doing in his closet, in his room, where he sat on Bernard Street, blocks and blocks from McDonald's? With a new hope, Johnny Tangle reached into his closet and pulled out an old dusty box which read, "The McDonald's Brand® Play-Doh Food Factory™." With reborn awareness, Johnny Tangle had a solution.

As he assembled the old factory, he smiled to himself. This was quite the educational experience; so, this is how they make McDonald's. They must have tons of these suckers in the back, just pumping out food. Johnny opened up the old canister, shocked that McDonald's was actually made out of Play-Doh. This was much more interesting than science class could ever be.

For the first time in his life, Johnny felt a sense of control as he put the Play-Doh through the factory. His mother didn't matter, Dally's indifference didn't matter, and the grossloaf certainly didn't matter. Johnny had a secret weapon buried right in his closet. Whenever he wanted McDonald's, he could have it.

The purple Grench fries didn't smell like McDonald's. Johnny feverishly checked over the box. There was Ronald, there were the arches, and even old Grimace was hanging out. It wasn't hot and greasy like McDonald's, either, and Johnny certainly didn't feel inclined to mindlessly devour it like he would if he were actually at McDonald's. The difference, however, is that this was his creation. Johnny wanted McDonald's, and Johnny found a way to make it happen. He held his Play-Doh hamburger carefully in his hand, with the attention a parent would bestow upon a newborn. This was his and it was beautiful.

Although Johnny quickly had produced his Play-Doh food, he

felt hesitant to eat it. Downstairs, he could hear his parents fighting over something, loud and cursing. It could be dinner, it could be Johnny. What he wanted, more than anything, was to show his parents the food he made. Maybe he could be making dinner every night? No more grossloaf, no more fighting. Johnny gripped his Play-Doh tightly, waiting to see his parents again, as he drifted off to sleep.

ELIZABETH WARREN AND THE DEATH OF MTV

"You smile like a cartoon, tooth for a tooth; you said that irony was the 'shackles of youth..."

If you're someone who likes getting the ending up front, I'll spare you the details: the hero of the story is Bill Berry. I had gotten a copy of R.E.M.'s *Automatic for the People* (1992) the week of its release—the cassette was yellow—and immediately fell in love with the record. While it would be years before I could appreciate the clever writing of singer Michael Stipe, the album served as a welcome departure from what I understood as music in the early 1990's. While Axl Rose and Metallica were producing work of equal measure, R.E.M. was my first exposure to the idea that things didn't always need to rock—R.E.M. wasn't afraid to give a moment space and allow a song to breath—this gave "Drive" room to brood ominously and "Everybody Hurts" time to emotionally settle. "Nightswimming" is still one of my favorite songs and always manages to make me cry.

As much as I loved the record at twelve years old, I had the awful hunch that I was being duped. I had thought of myself as a kind of emerging rock critic, a junior Robert Christgau compiling my own *Consumers Guide to Rock*; I knew what rocked and what sucked. But there was something fishy about 1992: *everything rocked*. Metallica put out their classic self-titled album the year prior. Guns and Roses had their epic *Use Your Illusion* double-shot. Nirvana and Nine Inch Nails were changing the rules of the game by the minute and getting anyone still using hairspray hooked on Xanax. Tori Amos released her beautiful debut, *Little Earthquakes* (1992), and further expanded upon what I thought of as music. Blind Melon had a hit single that was loved by all. Stone Temple

Pilots and Pearl Jam had incredible records. In every direction, there seemed to be the future of classic rock etching its name into the hollows of time.

But it all seemed too good to be true. Maybe I was too young to understand music; maybe the promotional forces behind the commercial success of the rock groups I loved were so strong and savvy that I wouldn't know the difference between rocking and sucking. What if there really wasn't anything special about any of this?

MTV was able to marry music and image in a way that wasn't possible before. Even if they didn't invent the music video, they presented it with aggression. In the channel's purest form, MTV was an assault on the senses. They kept their stars in heavy rotation; you'd lose count of how many times "Smells Like Teen Spirit" (1991) was shown in a single day. It was television programming without beginning or end—without shape or form—one that didn't necessitate undivided attention. It was something you'd be inclined to keep on all day, running in the background, feeding you a constant hum of subconscious messaging. The brand itself became a part of your identity; in 1992, it was cool to like MTV. Every rock group I liked in 1992 existed as a component of MTV.

The old-timers, your friend's dad with his collection of Zeppelin vinyl, would take shots at our beloved, monotheistic rock culture as being *too commercial*—a shot that stung, especially to a twelve-year-old bent on scraping through the commercial sheen of modern rock to access the reality underneath—increasingly worried there wasn't a reality to access. There was cross-talk, of course; we loved spinning his old Sabbath records—Iommi's guitar had an earthier crunch on vinyl—and he loved Alice in Chains and Pantera. Still, the presence of MTV—its watchful, deadened eye humming along in the background—had to be reckoned with.

To what extent did what I like reflect how I wanted to be perceived? Even if projecting an image wasn't the primary concern, it certainly existed as a welcome consequence. You wanted your choice in music to shape who you were. You imitated the admirable qualities of the rock star in order to shape your personality. MTV served as a starter kit in building an identity from the ground up.

***

As she daydreams, Elizabeth Warren can't help but imagine her face tear-stained and her eyes bloodshot. She never bought into being the hero of her own story. Only in fantasy can she come to terms with the reality she's desperate to hide. I get it. I used to have a reoccurring nightmare where I'd show up to elementary school in my underwear. I'd realize it midway through the day, horrified, glimpsing at my bare legs under the desk. Once I noticed, I knew others would, too.

I had a professor who encouraged us to share our nightmares, undoubtedly to farm masturbation material under the guise of something Freudian, something that became apparent after a girl in our class revealed that she often dreams of an aggressive man preventing her from urinating.[30] I relayed my underwear at school story, and he made a lame joke about "body shame." This was likely done, in retrospect, to curry favor with the pee girl; the college professor equivalent of giving me a wedgie and stuffing me in a locker.

But he was wrong; it was never about body shame, it was tied to a subconscious fear that my ineptitude will eventually catch up with me. This felt hauntingly inevitable. When a problem begins, it can be easily ignored; ignore it for long enough and it will grow into something encompassing and destructive.

Elizabeth was never invited to the cool kids' table. When she tried to get on the wavelength of the hip—*hold on a sec, I'm gonna get me a beer*—she could never find the right frequency. A craft that should have been honed in her college days, when a young girl looking foolish comes off as adorable, and any misunderstanding could be forgiven with a blushing giggle. But that ship had sailed long ago for Elizabeth, and she knew it, now finding her only solace in imagining herself sitting on the chest of Alexandria Ocasio-Cortez, stifling her breath, and dropping heavy fists into the bridge of her nose. Her sobbing cries alternating between "I never understood" and "don't fuck with me."

AOC understands that the new era of politician must seem relatable in a highly specific way. Young voters want to see *themselves* reflected in their politicians; no longer are politicians intended to be aspirational. They want their political representatives to participate in social media image management, which comprises the bulk of a millennial's daily activities.[31]

The authenticity put forth must be carefully crafted and controlled, a concept that AOC intrinsically understands and a language that Warren doesn't speak.

***

The transition from MTV to YouTube was ultimately a byproduct of Martin Luther's *Ninety-five Theses* (1517). This should have been something obvious to Warren, still trying to cater a heroic image to an MTV audience gone extinct. When Luther granted the average person a direct line to the Divine, his intent was to destroy the hierarchy of the church. It was here that hierarchy took a negative connotation, a ripple effect that we're still experiencing today.

The purpose of MTV was to define what was cool and sell you accessibility to it. The rock star sat at the top of the pop-culture hierarchy. This relationship was one-sided: you were meant to emulate the rock star who considered you a peasant. Arena rock culture is the modern day king's speech, where you're given commands, dressed down for not executing them to the king's liking, and finally given token bits of hollow praise. Paul Stanley tells you when to sit and stand, chastises you for being "too tired," taunts you with possibly ending the performance, and finally sends you home telling you that he loves your town.

Warren is still running on the old MTV arena rock formula; she wants to tell you the story and she expects you to believe it.

Alexandria Ocasio-Cortez understands that the path to power is no longer linear; a linear path comes across as alienating and fascist. Millennials don't want a rock star, they want an *anti-rock star*. They don't want someone to admire; they want someone who will make them feel comfortable. They want a politician who will wear sweatpants, admit that "adulting is hard," and eat processed food. The groupie-fucking, hotel room-destroying, controlled chaos of Axl Rose would only serve to upset and confuse them. The new authenticity is in selling you an admirable loser.

***

It's ironic that liking an R.E.M. record led to me questioning the authenticity of the entire system. They were probably the least likely rock group to skew inauthentic; in 2011 they quietly disbanded, believing they were creatively bankrupt and couldn't make another great album.

And this is where we circle back to Bill Berry, R.E.M.'s original drummer, who left the band in 1997 to become a farmer. Berry did not have a falling out with the other members, nor does he carry any ill will; he didn't like his career anymore, so he broke up with it. It was an integrity move. He was able to stand at the core of the machine and back away by choice, the ultimate in authenticity; an authenticity without the consciousness of managing perception, an authenticity without an ulterior motive. An authenticity entirely foreign to Elizabeth Warren. Bill Berry just needed some time alone (and he feels fine).

SUCCESS

"Offer me solutions, offer me alternatives, and I decline."

I had this incredible moment of contentedness while kissing Sarah in the backseat of my car. "Heroin" was playing on the radio. She had asked me if I thought her breasts were as big as I was expecting; that perhaps her nudes were deceptively angled, the old MySpace trick. She was so nervous I wouldn't like her that she needed to hold her wine glass with both hands to prevent spillage. This worsened when I told her to cut the shit with the sterile, first date, *getting-to-know-you* chit-chat; maybe the last bold move I'd ever make. She had to put the glass down entirely.

Once in my car, she sat up straight, arched her back, and asked again, somewhere between seductive and genuinely worried. I told her that I'd need a closer look and took the straps of her dress off her shoulders. And I had this moment, in the back seat of my car, of true connection. I liked her; dark hair and large breasts. Insecure and she didn't bother to hide it. A kindred spirit left behind by the dating market, looking for something real. This felt different. This felt special.

The day after Christmas, 2016, and you wondered if what you were experiencing was the beginning of the end.

Even then, we were late in the game. Any semblance of success had passed for the well-intentioned, common man. Meeting Sarah was like catching a shooting star on your camcorder; standing in the right place at the right time and having the prescience to hit record on gut instinct alone. It could have been anyone, but it was you on the evening news, with a goofy smile, proudly showing your footage.

Success is hollow in a world without sex. You become the kid selling candy bars for a 13-inch color TV out of the prize catalog. If you take the idea of having nice kitchen appliances purchased to impress women out of the equation, it turns out you don't need very much. A notebook and a pen. A freezer full of meat and heavy things to push around. A car with enough gas in the tank to drive yourself to death when the time comes.

Dark thoughts. A text from Amazon cuts the tension. Your package is nine stops away; a blu-ray copy of *Ghostbusters II* (1989).[32] How could you have lived with this hole in your collection?

You get through another day.

The trick is to recalibrate: *redefine* success. Make money less relevant. Work for sustenance. Bitcoin was a psy-op to keep your type in line, you're sure. False hope for those ready to unplug and get off the grid. A hundred acres in Montana with your Bitcoin wife, starting a Bitcoin family, watching your net worth skyrocket effortlessly. "I think they call it *passive income*," you tell your no-coin friends who wouldn't listen. Entire notebooks of writing to be found when you're gone; to be cherished or burned, you'll never know.

It wasn't meant to work out. There's a power structure in place so deeply invested in the prevention of a new world order that any deviation would be the equivalent of breaking a law of nature, as much a fantasy as comic book superheroes. Believing in anything but an inevitable status-quo path to destruction is like standing in an arcade pumping quarters into *Donkey Kong* (1981); no way to win the game, but stand there long enough and you'll make it to the kill screen.

So you redefine success. You work within the system. You rearrange things quietly, when the warden isn't looking. Removing women as the end-goal presents such a radical freedom that it's shamed by the mainstream culture; men aren't meant to be free. You don't understand this because everything you've ever done was in the interest of getting women. True freedom is to excise this tumor and see what's left. Committing to this fully is the only way you'll ever get laid again, so it's win-win.

Letting go is the foundation; expression is the goal.

Not success.

Artists shouldn't be successful and success is antithetical to art is what you tell yourself. As you grind away, producing your best work to a "modest audience of dedicated readers," sacrificing sleep and sex. I'd pass on getting laid to write an essay on Elizabeth Warren, a string of words no one has put together before in human history. Madness by any other measure, but an artist must be obsessed with the creation of art. Success only muddies the waters, becoming a barrier between the artist and his work.

Success is toxic and must be avoided, says the unsuccessful.

Metallica was never the same after selling a billion copies of the *Black Album*. They were burdened by expectation, to replicate what worked and magnify those elements times infinity. The self-conscious artist is doomed to fail, betraying the instincts that led to their success. After the follow-up was met with a fraction of the sales, the band flailed wildly—chasing approval like desperate drunkards—culminating in a documentary where they all cry.

Modern men have no war to fight, so modernity has taken arms against us. The herd must be thinned. There are deep, esoteric reasons for why even fat women won't reply to your messages now on Plenty of Fish. Men have become weak and nature hit the emergency brakes. Now only the most genetically fit will get easy sex; for everyone else, the long game has gotten so long that it's no longer worth playing. To think that clever banter could have gotten you laid five years ago is astounding; to think that ambitious nerds had girlfriends in high school 20 years ago is the stuff of legend.

In 1992, schlock rock metal band GWAR put out their relative masterpiece, *America Must Be Destroyed*, but they were right for the wrong reasons. They argued that the country was naturally heading toward a wonderful, degenerate utopia but getting stifled by a gatekeeping Christian majority, a laughable take in hindsight.

Now when Tom likes Mindy at the office, he doesn't sidle up to her at the water cooler angling for Friday night drinks, but instead navigates to her premium Snapchat, his only hesitation in potential budgetary constraint. Maybe then, through private message—her response enticed by gifts purchased from her Amazon wish list—can he offer drinks? No, he decides this sounds too pedestrian. She already has rogue millionaires—those who got into Bitcoin when you were too lazy to scan your driver's license into an exchange—offering her weekends in Vegas. He needs to go big budget, if only he could after all the high-end kitchen appliances he purchased to impress her.

Impossible to talk to her at work, he concedes, as he settles for gawking at her tits for $25/month under the pseudonym *SneakyTim*, a necessary complication is his long-con courting game plan. There must be a slow reveal, the bandages must be removed with patience; any haste in the reveal that Tom is, in fact, a loyal subscriber with a commendable accumulation of gifts purchased anonymously would result in a swift #MeToo accusation and the loss of all present and future employment. Moves must be made with gentle and conscientious precision, thinks SneakyTim, as he sends Mindy the requisite $50 for her long-form masturbation video; for *fans only*, of course.

The problem isn't a prudish morality, but I can't blame GWAR for being wrong. They acknowledged the problem; that the modern world is diseased beyond salvation. All valid modern art must stem from this foundation. The cocaine addled *brat pack* of young, hip authors couldn't get past the nihilism of 1980's party culture. The excess of sex and drugs. The tail end of the KISS concert, with its fireworks and confetti, was the payoff for what was built by the Boomers, its spectacular finale. They were overfed hamsters, rolling around in their own filth.

The modern writer was sold the promise of decadence and pays the debt of decay.

The silence felt awkward. I knew my mistake the moment I had made it; it sat cold and moist on the upper part of my thigh. We were getting to know each other now as if what we had was in the past tense, like a post-game show on ESPN. She spoke without the constraint of keeping in character, telling me how she had dated a rock star as a teenager and about her abusive ex-boyfriend.

Women don't respect condom use. Even if you're still fucking her, it's the shareware version of the full product. *Limited functionality*. They'll always hesitate before conceding; you must anticipate this and remain strong in your resolve. I had a good run before Sarah, but like an aging fighter, I got caught with a roundhouse in a moment of weakness.

"Sorry I'm such a slut," read her text message the next day. Her way of tying things up. You're left wondering what the best case scenario would have been or if this was it.

So you redefine success. You realize the value in dwelling at the epicenter. You retch at the idea of becoming complacent, spouting naiveté like you're handing out recipe cards to the secret sauce. You're resigned to staring at the sun. You create art with a high degree of authenticity. You put integrity before all else. You never write with consideration for the reader, and you find that even the promotion of your own work has minor hints of insincerity, just like the minor hints of dark chocolate and citrus in your favorite cold-brew coffee blend; not pronounced, but *palpable*.

People will find this approach refreshing. Your work will effortlessly find an audience. You've created a beautiful middle ground between honesty and success; degrees of integrity you didn't think were possible. Those in the mainstream take notice and resent your defiant take on modern life. Your popularity continues to grow. You appear on podcasts; people analyze your material. Your follower count on Twitter makes panties wet.[33] Hundreds of retweets for a few scant words. You title an essay "The Modern Rock Star," referring to yourself, but are never quite brazen enough to publish. You feel bulletproof.

And then, one day, your tweets are blown-up on a poster board in front of Congress. *The Huffington* Post publishes your most unflattering pictures. "Ashamed" is the keyword most repeated in your mother's interview with the *New Yorker*.

Success.

DAWN OF THE DEAD

"And I used to be strong, I used to be tough, and she used to be pretty, but now she's just pretty fucked up."

She told me that she never likes the ones who call her pretty. A mistake made in earnest, a fleeting desire for something real, not acting out a teenage roleplay with an aging woman over cheap drinks. When the fantasy is all that's left, the impulse is to get lost in it. You want to forget that you're an arm above the water and your legs are giving out.

You want this to be what it isn't; it's been too long and you're too far from the shore. You want to pretend that you've lucked out and the prom queen agreed to a Saturday night at the drive-in. That isn't what this is, and you know it, but it's more satisfying to spend time pretending rather than going through the motions where you say the right words at the right times, like you're punching in a Nintendo code, to skip to the end and pump rockets into Mother Brain.

Better get out before the whole thing explodes.

She doesn't want you to think she's pretty. That's not part of her fantasy and her fantasy is all that matters. This is your first date, and you're a sucker if you let her think you like her. She wants to feel your contempt. She wants to think you were busy with a girl ten years younger the night before and that she'd be lucky to suck your dick. She wants to work for it. She wants someone who hates her. This was your shot and you blew it.

This is what you get for being single at 40. Meaning dies the further you get from your teenage years until you're whisked off into the middle of the ocean to drown. Middle-aged women read books about being brave while starting inspirational Instagram pages; men learn the right words to say, in the right order, to get to the end of the game. If you're looking for meaning in any of this, you lose.

Teenage love is only real for you to stick around long enough to make sure the girl you knocked up isn't eaten by bears. It's evolutionary. You're a tool for the survival of your people, and you're dropped like a rock when you're too old to be useful. You're the walking dead—a vampire—and if you dare look for meaning you'll be starved out of existence. Only the savvy get laid here, bucko, so get with the program or learn to go hungry.

A genuine moment of breathless eye-contact feels like a lifetime ago. Now everything has the sheen of production. You know exactly how long to wait before looking away, the right pauses to take, how to use your breath; you're ten times sexier, but even the moments that you want to come off as genuine are only performative. Once you sell your integrity, it's gone for good.

The rock band reunion is a misnomer. Their legacy is cemented in time; anything else is something new and different. The reunion *matters less*; people get old, things get muddled. Why even bother? You can't capture the innocence of the original—the moment that hung in the air like an eternal sunrise—you can only exploit it. You take what you've learned about women and use it to fuck them. That's the game, Vlad. You've become a cannibal in a world where you either learn the rules of the dead or sit on your hands thinking you're pious. Guess what, no one cares.

You had your shot at a story and you blew it. In another time, in another life, you'd have that two-car garage. Where are the kids now, kung-fu soccer? She keeps her phone face down because she spends her nights *reconnecting* with friends from high school on Facebook. Don't worry, Kevin's married now, too, but she doesn't want you to get the *wrong idea*. You had your shot at a story and you blew it. You're not Scott Weiland, you're Jeff Gutt. The real singer ODed and you're just the replacement, so shut up and sing "Plush."

Pretty like an aging Barbie doll is what you tell her. You've realized your misstep and all you've got left is a Hail Mary neg, but the damage has been done. You called her pretty and now you're not going to fuck her. This will bother you for the rest of your life; you'll lie in bed, jacking off to the idea. Because you couldn't fuck her, she's ten times hotter than any girl you've ever fucked, and you'll be chasing that ghost forever.

You're Dave Mustaine and what could have been will always matter more than what was. Nothing you have will ever compare to the ones who got away. You can't tolerate hearing "no." You have inexplicable confidence. You're incredibly entitled. You think everyone should be kissing your ass.

Even if you have a sold out club with people chanting your name, you spot the one guy in the "Delicious Tacos" T-shirt and have security kick him out; Tacos is playing the hockey arena down the street, buddy. "Better to reign in Hell" is what you tell yourself to justify your fragile ego. Say no to me and it's a lifetime of masturbation, dream girl; hope you can deal with that.

She'll never know, and she'll never think of you again because you called her pretty instead of making her feel like shit.

2019

"Faster than the speed of sound...faster than we thought we'd go..."

For most of last year, I enjoyed getting to work an hour before everyone else. Often, I'd be the first in the building, the motion lights of the vacant hallways clicking to life upon my arrival. It felt important to settle into work. As I age, my brain seems to take longer and longer to heat up; like one of those old IBM computers, with the turbo button on the yellowing plastic shell, that would only display green type on a black screen. Back when computers held mysteries and nerds were the only priestly caste who could access them. Now computers are vehicles for advertisements and nerds are the people happiest about it.

I enjoyed getting to work early because the roads were empty and I could speed. The highway I'd choose was wonderfully twisted, lined with trees, and toward the end of the school year, my backdrop would become a gorgeous sunrise. It felt like playing *OutRun* (1986) and just the idea that a wrong move could flip my Honda Accord (I chose the "sports model") and send it bouncing across the road made me feel alive. The only risk embedded in my daily routine was cut short by a speeding ticket. The officer was polite and reduced my 78 in a 55 to a 75 citing major differences in consequence. I appreciated that. I plead guilty by mail and got a reasonably prompt reply that my guilty plea was rejected. A court date was to be determined.

But I wouldn't get to work early to do *actual work*; it was genuinely about swimming through lanes to cut off the guy doing 65 in the left. Send him a message about my superiority. Maybe an intervention of sorts; only the strong survive. Feel the torque of your pickup and become who you are.

Pac-Man chasing ghosts, viciously cutting off anyone who considers safety an inherent guarantee of highway usage, watching in the rearview as they drift to the right. Lesson learned.

I'd get to work and watch old MTV videos on YouTube. Stuff you couldn't have fully appreciated upon initial airing. When I got to *1979* (1996), I found myself watching on repeat, my eyes welling with tears, in what would become my morning ritual for the rest of the year.

There's a complexity to adolescence that becomes forgotten in adulthood. Like the ability to truly fall in love, once it's lost, it's gone forever. People who shit on adolescence—who mock those who miss high school, who swear they'd never go back while laughing at the cynicism they've developed over the years—are dead inside and should be avoided. If you're so far gone that you can't remember a time more lofty and wistful… you may as well give yourself over to the system entirely, work your bullshit job until you're dead, and, if you're a woman, get pounded out by every shithead with a decent opener on Plenty of Fish. Most men don't have that luxury. If you do have fond memories of adolescence, you'll end up doing all that just the same, but at least you're not an asshole.

Adolescence is the intersection of childhood freedom and adult responsibility. Childhood isn't terribly interesting, even when romanticized, and being an adult is like a sitcom that's been running for infinite seasons too long—every year a rehash of the same—everything amplified to parody, where Kramer and George are building a rocket ship out of couch cushions because George got caught masturbating at the library. The manifestation of sexuality is what makes the human experience interesting, but too much sexuality gets old quickly. There is nothing romantic about a 22-year-old trying to fuck everything that moves; in another time, in another place, that energy could have been harnessed to build bridges and craft beauty, but in Hell, we spill fluid on hormonally-altered women and consider that success.

But there's a beauty to the emerging sexuality of adolescence. Taking a closer look at the pool scene in *1979*, we find the play and exploration of childhood, as a boy and girl leave a house party to hop the fence of a neighbor and swim in their in-ground pool, before a fleeting moment of eye-contact becomes a welcome kiss. There's a moment where the girl smiles with elation and—as if this was too much, too soon—the characters are next seen throwing patio furniture into the pool; a regression to the aimless destruction of suburban living.

There's a greater depth of meaning to that kiss than every OkCupid date you've ever been on. In a perfect world, they'll marry and share variations of that kiss for the rest of their lives, evolving as they mature—taking the form of spending the first night in their new house, giving the first bath to their newborn daughter, the disastrous first Thanksgiving they host—everything carrying the newness of that kiss, and for a lifetime, they'll never step out of that moment.

A moment that's been erased by the modern world, a moment that's become as dreamlike as a music video. A modern world where people don't marry young, a modern world that's given us the gift of college life and travel, exploration and experience, time on our side with a double middle finger aimed at anyone who doesn't get the joke; that we're too good to replicate the lives of our parents, too good for our fuck count to be in the single digits, too good to marry our high school sweethearts, and only once that it's too late to change course, as we careen down the highway—swimming through lanes and cutting off cars—will we understand that we'll be chasing those ghosts forever.

THIS SPACE BETWEEN US

"These weeds have grown where the sun once shown..."

It used to bother me thinking I didn't exist outside of how others perceived me. The moments I spent alone, while significant to me, felt shapeless, as if what's experienced in solitude existed on a plane between dream and fiction. The inner world can only be represented in close approximation, and that representation is all that exists; you are who others perceive you to be. No one is interested in you beyond the value of your public face.

You are nothing.

The coldness of deep space.

In *Videodrome* (1983), they had the homeless watch television—the most pragmatic form of charity—food and shelter would only be a temporary fix. The socially discarded—those without a public face, who no longer exist—can only be brought back to life learning the etiquette of public existence. Erase the lunacy of authenticity—speaking without a veil is feral behavior—your personality needs a high degree of digestibility. Good morning, America, *Coke is it*.[34] Like that.

Only that isn't it; it's a starting point. The difference between something and nothing; being "patched back into the world's mixing board" and existing as a walking corpse. Social intelligence is acting within the scope of acceptability while pretending as though you aren't, that you're the brand, the influencer, and the genesis of memes. Even if the counterculture is where you find yourself settling—the alternative, Pepsi instead of Coke, or RC-fucking-Cola for the real crazies—there is still a mixing board to find and a set of unspoken rules to follow, with only a small allowance for authenticity.

The greater degree to which you're able to find *originality* within the narrow band of acceptability, the higher degree of social intelligence you'll be regarded with. Making a Borat joke at a party in 2020 isn't exactly a *faux pas*, but would serve as a dog whistle to anyone hipper than you that you aren't part of the club; making an Austin Powers reference, even worse. When aging content creators don't understand how they were left behind, it's that the unspoken language of the mixing board changed without their notice.

"We are who we choose to be," is what the Green Goblin tells Spider-Man.[35] The recurring theme of *Master of Puppets* (1986) is how little control we have over these choices, manipulated by forces from both outside and within. Tyler Durden thought it better to be defined by destruction if the only other choice is consumption. To Shane Carruth, our identity is shaped in ways that are so distant—so far *upstream*—that they're unknowable. When Laura Loomer was kicked off the Internet, she was pulled away from the only reality she had come to know. A bag of guts resembling Laura Loomer cried and screamed on talk shows, threatened suicide, and handcuffed herself to an office building, but none of that mattered, because Loomer was already dead. If the self is meaningless when not translated to a language that can be understood by the other, then Laura Loomer was erased. She'll survive, but she'll need to become someone new—a different mixing board, a new set of social rules—but one without all the Twitter followers and attention. Only she can answer whether that's a life worth living.

***

The decade of peak American excess pushed with vigor the idea that all people should be photogenic while simultaneously eating a diet of processed foods. This is what was considered progress; beauty and convenience. Of course, these ideas existed at odds with one another, which brought the diet industry to the forefront of American life. No longer were already trim girls chasing an ideal and a husband—now obese Americans were playing catch-up, and late-night infomercials promising beauty and convenience were there to exploit them—this is where Richard Simmons enters the story.

Simmons may have sold different products over the years, from

Deal-a-Meal to *Sweatin' to the Oldies*, but really, Simmons *himself* was the product. Simmons had tremendous charisma that popped off the screen; a ball of kinetic energy who was constantly screaming with joy or breaking down in tears depending on what the situation called for. Most of all, Simmons conveyed an incredible sense of *authenticity*—when he cried, relaying his own struggles with self-image, you knew he'd understand you—when he shouted that you too could do it, you believed him.

It's easy to think that Simmons was the ultimate used car salesman, but the curveball to the story is the friendships he formed with clients along the way. Simmons would meet obese women, desperate and depressed, and provide free personal coaching—which turned into soft-therapy—which often became late-night phone-calls with Simmons having his own emotional breakdowns, needing his own support; these relationships went both ways. Similarly, Simmons would use his exercise studio—Slimmons, where he would personally lead classes for $12 per session—as a form of group therapy. His breakdowns, and the resulting sweaty hugs, became a part of the experience.

And then one day, Richard Simmons disappeared.

He stopped making talk show appearances. He stopped teaching at Slimmons. He stopped coaching obese women over the phone. He stopped talking to friends. He stopped leaving his house.

Richard Simmons stopped being Richard Simmons.[36]

It's easy to think that this serves as proof that Simmons was a fraud—a late-night infomercial hustler—using the perception of authenticity to make millions. Maybe he needed the ego fluffing of obese women in Middle America being dependent on his phone calls and his friendship. Maybe he felt safe using them for his own therapy, late at night, when there was no one around to perform for. What seems more likely is that Richard Simmons couldn't be Richard Simmons anymore. The animating spirit that embodied the bag of guts that became known as Richard Simmons had left the body, and this public face had become so strong that Simmons was effectively dead without it. All that existed was the public face and now there is nothing left.

***

There's a tangible feeling when things are slipping away with someone.

It happens so gradually that the bits of progression toward the end, taken individually, are mostly invisible—only at the end does it all come together like an Agatha Christie novel—but if you close your eyes and reach out with your feelings, it's all there, certainly in retrospect. She doesn't respond to you like she did; she doesn't have the same look in her eyes. These were things so strong and immediate at the beginning that you could have almost touched them.

Sex with her had felt choreographed. I guess they call that chemistry. The way our mouths would move in sync; the way our bodies would entwine. Flowing from the bed to having her pressed against the wall in what felt like a single motion; the softness in her eyes during the pauses we'd take from kissing.

Your act will become a parody of itself by the third month. You become Bob Crane flubbing his lines while doing dinner theater. To you, it's all the same, but the audience will notice. By the time she was mirroring my pout, repeating my signature *"Baby..."* with exaggerated emphasis, I should have known it was over. Dates went from fucking all night while forgetting about dinner, to fucking before dinner dates because who wants sex after? All deliberate clues that the attentive reader would only catch on a second go-through; things indistinguishable the first time around.

I made up for my Christmas gag of only getting her gifts that were actually for me—the plaid mini-skirt, the perfume I wanted her to wear—by making Valentine's Day selfless. A hand-written love letter and a movie gift card for her and her daughter where they could "talk about how great I am," I joked in the letter. When she took the envelope, she had a minor look of terror as she felt it thoroughly for the outline of a ring. Another bit of foreshadowing; now you know why Mrs. White had the candlestick in the study.

The last time I saw her, I asked her to see me again. One last time would change things. "Why," she asked. "What would that do?"

And, with that, we were strangers again. Slowly, over time, the person she had known disappeared. I had become a bag of guts wasting her time on a Wednesday night. I discarded the script we were using and started to ad-lib my own. I unplugged from our mixing board and fell too deeply into the lunacy of authenticity.

I had stopped being me.

DON'T FEAR THE REAPER

"Baby, I'm your man."

Nothing ends well. I hate to be the one to tell you, but if you didn't already know, romantic endings are for Hollywood. Real life wouldn't have made it past a single test screening. I've never watched someone die, and my hands carry the softness of a man with intellectual savvy; I've never known hard labor and this is something I appreciate. After I scrub diligently for 20 seconds and dry thoroughly, I enjoy the soft touch of my fingertips on my reasonably ageless face. People are shocked that I'm 40, and with a baseball cap turned slightly askew, I can still fuck reasonably young women.

But this isn't going anywhere. The joke is that once you hammer out the formula, in your Henry Frankenstein fuck laboratory, you're already halfway bored by the results. They say the journey is more satisfying than the destination, but once you've slipped into the realm of hindsight, you wonder if that's just another bit of Hollywood bullshit. You have so many of the same interactions that it all blurs together and becomes part of your muscle memory—like realizing *Punch-Out* (1987) is a rhythm game—you could do it blindfolded. You thought you were Tony Soprano, a playboy with a dark side, but you're really Livia; "it's all a big nothing," something you understand now more than you ever thought you would.

So you resign yourself to wanting something real. You think you've finally come up with the right equation for it, and even if you understand the immutable fact that *genuine relationships don't exist in Hell*, you're still going out to slay demons with your spear and armor until you get the girl, even if you have to play through the game twice.

But nothing ends well. Hollywood endings are called that for a reason. I never took my dog for the walk I was too busy for before his liver failed.[37] You won't say the right things to resolve the years of tension you've had with your parents before they die, even if you come close. You won't find the right girl to ride off into the sunset with: "all a big nothing."

When Nancy told me that she wasn't sure how she felt, I knew it was time to go. You never want to get jobbed out of a territory; the idea is to leave on your own accord. It was time to go, and I told her I wasn't going to stay the night, something that struck a nerve with her. She felt comfortable sussing out her feelings in language that could hang in the air and be arranged and rearranged like refrigerator magnets. This was the kind of control she expected; her *decision* and her *terms*. But the ultimate sin in a relationship is forgetting that it's a perpetual game of chess; even when it feels like it isn't, there's no rest for the wicked.

I was sincere in leaving. I collected my things and she walked me to the door, where I took one last look at her. I thought she was beautiful, another sin when you're living in Hell, and took a second to linger. I wanted to feel something. You want to feel a goodbye.[38] It may be the last time you ever feel anything remotely close to love for a woman, even if this were only in bite-sized pieces with artificial flavoring; love adjacent, maybe.

You wait to feel something, but what you want is acknowledgment that she's there with you in the moment. You want a look of presence in her eyes. Only men are fools enough to get caught up in nostalgia—romanticizing the past—women are too pragmatic for that. Like hungry wolves, they understand picking bones and moving on. Cut out at the right time, and she'll still care; you'll get that look in her eyes, and you'll feel your goodbye.

I told her I'd see her around; saying goodbye felt too real. She had a moment of fluster, a minor stutter when she'd get too nervous, then smiled and said, "Maybe at Target," a joke we shared, that I was always running into ex-girlfriends at Target. I took another pause, touched her face, returned her smile, and left.

So perfect an ending to tidy up a good-enough six months that I would have been able to reflect fondly on it for years; so perfect that it couldn't have really been the end. If endings seem too emotionally charged, you end up going back to them. Things only truly die in cancer-ravaged hospital beds; black and stinking, shit and piss.

That's *actual reality*, not storybooks; not Hollywood. The zombie invasion end-of-the-world scenario, where we go out defending civilization with homemade weapons and combat cars, was never going to happen. A global pandemic is the reality we deserve—death by the neoliberal consumer hellscape we created—death by Amazon Prime, death by Travelocity—death by wanderlust, death by modern sin—holed up in our homes, being lied to by our governments while our lungs collapse. There is no perfect goodbye.

We saw each other until that look in her eyes was gone. That's reality; you drive a relationship into the ground trying to make it work, trying to play catch-up, and you go out counting the lights. You realize it's over two weeks too late, and your last memory of her is only coldness, all a big nothing, and you'd better get used to it.

SOME TIME ALONE

"And I'm in so deep; you know I'm such a fool for you. You've got me wrapped around your finger. Do you have to let it linger?"

She kissed my cheek and excused herself to the bathroom. Alone in Dana's bedroom, I walked over to the shelf with her wedding picture. My peripheral vision had picked up on this when I entered the room; my eyes developed the keenness of a hunter. Her husband had finally moved out that morning, she told me. Time to party.

Two weeks since I'd sent a text that read "no one fucking breaks up with me," a few days after which I was sitting in the backseat of my car with Janine on my lap, hunched over with her arms around my neck and the small of her back pressed against the driver's seat, my hands in her hair and her breath on my cheek, as she sang along to "Pretty Good Year" while quietly crying. Puzzle pieces that would've seemed foreign to anyone who walked in late, who didn't see her response to things I'd written that resonated with her, who didn't see the video she took of herself singing "Linger" with the word *fucking* inserted in the chorus—a little something I always thought would intensify the emotional impact of the song—just to impress me.

She texted me to meet her in a coffee shop where she was working on her graduate thesis. Before the world ended, this made sense. She asked about different pieces I'd written; she was fascinated. This is what you get for writing things that aren't repulsive to women; something, I guess, every other writer instinctively understands. Why do anything that doesn't get you sex? I've always been a slow learner.

I wanted to know about her life. This was the wrong move if I wanted sex, but I guess I'd rather write than get laid after all. Slow learner. She told me that she met a guy on Ashley Madison, and after a few months of talking, she left her husband. Turns out the guy was a liar and he ditched her, but her husband was still a pussy, so she wasn't going back; she was left emotionally homeless. This is where I enter the story. She'd been married since her early twenties; never cheated until she met the new guy and never experienced heartbreak either. Her lips were cold when we kissed. She cried about being abandoned as she silently plotted to find her way back.

She thought she was tricked into falling in love, but this is as real as it gets in Hell. You experience a few perfect moments that you want to keep, but they always manage to sneak away as you're settling in. Love is allowing these moments to pass. Acknowledge that you have nothing and it won't be such a shock to find out that you don't get to keep anything.

Her husband moved out that morning, and Dana didn't want to spend the night alone. She texted me to meet at her house where she had spent the day drinking. I was settling into my own evening—the sun had gone down and my dinner was almost ready—but these are opportunities you've learned to never turn down. Be positive; come from a place of yes. It didn't feel as adventurous as it would have just a few years prior, but you weren't going to let the world's inertia drop any hints. You still felt young, and young men don't turn down sex: they go on adventures.

After a few minutes of the kind of small talk that Japanese businessmen make before trying to slit each other's throats, she kissed me in her kitchen before leading me to her bedroom and excusing herself to the bathroom.

No one fucking breaks up with me is what I texted her. I don't do well when situations spiral out of my control. Axl Rose wrote "One in a Million" when he bought into the idea that rock stars were bulletproof and wanted to test that theory, and when the results came back negative, with a media backlash, he tanked his own band. A control freak won't play the game when he can't make the rules. Rose reemerged 20 years later with an album examining the limits of control; *Chinese Democracy* (2008) was only a metaphor.

No one fucking breaks up with me, and when they do, you escalate with napalm. Time alone is for suckers; you don't mourn what's dead, you watch the corpse burn in the rearview. You meet girls that fucking weekend, *that fucking night*—as many as you can—and use every bit of charm that she took for granted, that you know she's going to miss, and you make every girl you meet pay for her letting you go. You drink at night and write about it, examining things from all angles. You were too good to her, you made things too easy for her, she didn't know what she had and she threw it all away. Axl Rose spent 20 years writing about being taken for granted, abandoned; no one fucking breaks up with him.

No one fucking breaks up with me, and you don't care, because you did. Now I'm waiting for a stranger to finish pissing, to have sex with, to spite you. Looking at her wedding picture on the shelf in her bedroom, I wonder if she's meeting me for the very same reason.

DATING AND REALITY (PICNIC, LIGHTNING)

"The only convincing love story of our century."[39]

Like getting a glimpse of a video game's final boss moments before your own destruction, unless you're a real stud, you never get much experience having threesomes. Those who romanticize it have either never done it or done it so many times that listening to them in the first place would be like taking financial advice from a trust-fund kid. *It's nice to be rich.* But outside of a resume piece that only comes up in the screening interviews you have with new women you're trying to fuck, who'll assume you're lying anyway, or a sexual bucket list that you only understand as meaningless once it's all checked off, threesomes are mostly silly.

This is the reality that every Internet guru, selling you thousands of dollars of bullshit and filming those ridiculous-looking three-way kisses at foam parties in Cancun, will gladly lie about.

Her name was Candace. We met her on Craigslist. I wrote the ad for my girlfriend to post; I had her screen the replies, and she'd have the decent ones text me. We had a good cop/bad cop dynamic; she was friendly with these women, I was demanding. Candace had a boyfriend, but he was too nice; he lacked grit. She liked that I was in my thirties dating a 19-year-old. This is what women say they hate, and maybe they do on some level, but they're lying if they say they don't find it intriguing. After all, what kind of 34-year-old is dating a teenager? The kind they want to fuck.

As much as the girlfriend tells you that she's okay with everything, seducing another girl in front of her is going to feel strange. Don't forget to take mental pictures because this will be the best part of the evening. You watch them make out, and you feel accomplished; you created this and *it is good*—now you know what it feels like to be God—but anything after is an awkward mesh of bodies. I defy anyone to find a good way to do this.

I came on her face thinking about how fucking awful it all was; sending her home to her boyfriend after she met some dipshit on Craigslist. The hot shower she'd have to take before getting in bed and acting like it was ladies' night at Barnes and Noble; just coffee and chit chat with the girls, *that's all*. I couldn't decide whether I wanted her to be masturbating in the shower or crying, but one of the two seemed inevitable, maybe both.

And when she finally leaves to take that shower, you feel a tinge of existential horror. You take a beat to wonder why you did it in the first place; what were you looking to get out of fucking a stranger in front of your girlfriend? Threesome is a misnomer; it isn't chaotic like *Final Fight* (1989), it's slower and turn-based like *Final Fantasy* (1990). Did you really just do it to say you did it? This thought haunts you.

You all shared the experience, but you each saw something different. You were bent on validation, having something to prove after hitting rock bottom several years prior, breaking your engagement, and returning to the world of the living, but now your victory lap felt flat. Candace was rebelling against a boring boyfriend with the most scandalous and pornographic scenario she could find. Your kid girlfriend was dipping her toes into what she presumed the adult world would be like, maybe after too much time on the Internet, too much time watching cable TV.

We were all there for different reasons, and none of them were genuine; we did it just to say we did it. We were objects to one another, and each used the other to reach their own end. The sex was necessary but ultimately perfunctory. This bothered me for a few moments before I jacked off and went to bed.

If you couldn't guess, having a kid girlfriend is fucking hilarious. If you're riding a wave of indignation, where you suddenly feel righteous flipping a double bird to the world around you, there is no better way to do it. People will stare, and if you're not ready to play it like a bad guy pro wrestler, this type of social norm-bucking isn't for you, and maybe you're the guy waiting at home while she's doing "girls' night at the bookstore." The married couple with the stroller will shoot dirty looks, but you'll catch hubby stealing a glimpse of her ass every time. The blue-haired checkout girl at Target won't hide her disgust; the lonely boy working the deli counter at the grocery store will stare longingly, another dagger through his heart.

She was here on loan from down south. Got a gig as a live-in babysitter. The dad would try to get with her when the mom wasn't around; the perks of having hired help, I guess. She moved in with me after she quit and we spent two weeks bouncing around Mexico to celebrate. Guys would try to hit on her thinking I was her father. We'd drink liquor in the ocean by moonlight and laugh at anyone who didn't get the joke. We were living in our own world and writing the rules for it as we went along.

Once you realize that men are the only ones held to a social standard and women are given a pass for morally gray behavior, you're happy to tell the whole system to fuck off. When your fiancée's father sits you down and gives you a speech about male responsibility, which translates strictly to *paying my daughter's bills,* and the open-ended question that hangs in the air, never to be addressed, is "what should the man expect out of the deal?", what you can expect to hear are crickets.

So men on the street suckered in by lecherous wives, blue-haired retail employees emboldened by a system happy to endlessly masturbate them, I invite you to stare at a man who's found freedom in not giving a fuck.

A month later, we took off to rural Washington state on a hiking trip where I rented the biggest truck I could find and we climbed mountains and picked blueberries in deep solitude. Marijuana had just been legalized, so we loaded up on pre-rolled joints and spent our evenings getting high in the Jacuzzi tub, and I've never felt more alone in my life.

So far out in the sticks that the nearest fast food place was staffed by happy people and your meal looked like the picture on the poster. Hundreds of miles from civilization, thousands from home. Far enough away that you didn't have any rules left to defy. Far enough away to realize that you were two different people with absolutely nothing in common. She couldn't hope to understand you, and you never bothered to try to understand her; the *real her,* the genuine her, beyond what you wanted her to represent. She was an object to you, and now, in total isolation, it became pressing and urgent.

You're so high that you confide in her the horror you feel watching your parents get old; you've always known what was inevitable, but you've only recently begun to feel it. This angers her; you aren't supposed to have feelings, you were never supposed to be a fully-realized person. You were always the embodiment of a fantasy—the older man—as a sex object and father figure. She wanted you to stay that way.

We never saw each other as people; we were only flat images to one other, caricatures on a page, reduced to our defining features, exaggerated and cartoonish. We never saw each other as people; we only saw what we wanted.[40]

BETTER TO REIGN IN HELL

"I dressed up in scarecrow, she dressed up in white..."

She told me that she likes "fuckboys," a terrible, disingenuous cope of a nomenclature, a way for women to reclaim power in an otherwise powerless situation, thinking that, in our modern landscape of gender equality, a slur designed for a man who has too much sex will have the same sting as one made to shame women; fuckboys, she said, because she likes the way they talk to her. She was over 40 with three kids; when she ditched the hubby, she got herself a personal trainer and breast implants, which was probably the most sensible thing to do. Ride the midnight train out as far as it will go; better to have your pick of fuckboys than to get a look at the kind of loser who'd take you seriously.

She had fake tits, so I felt compelled to continue the conversation. Breast implants are sexy for everything but their aesthetic value; they rarely look good, with the exception being implants that look so good you'd never know they were fake, surely a secret taken to the grave, but typically they're closer to bad 90's porn. There's an unspoken symbolic value to fake tits, signaling an intense vanity combined with a deep comfort in promiscuity, where even if her tits are fake, her willingness to exist as a sex doll is more real than any woman with "no hookups, not looking for a one-night stand" written in at the bottom of her dating profile. There's a refreshing purity to this approach; only a woman with fake tits will tell you that she likes fuck boys.

People would rather hear bullshit than anything genuine. KISS floundered in obscurity, bankrupting their record label with their most sincere and artistic work, that all bombed commercially until they released a live record that hit big and made them celebrities. Since their live shows were packed and their studio albums were duds, why not go into the studio to record a live album; a total fake, disconnected from the performances that made their act a success.[41] *Alive!* (1975) bore little difference from their already recorded studio material; the same songs with a bed of crowd noise ripped from Monday Night Football. This is what people want; people want you to lie.

***

If you want to know her number—her real number—you need to approach the conversation delicately. If you lead with how you're "sick of the sluts on Plenty of Fish"—land of the washed-up party girl—she's going to throw you a number impossibly low for a single girl over 40. You could take a beat, close your eyes, and allow yourself to believe the lie—you could let this narrative form the foundation of a relationship, your own personal mythology—two crazy kids who finally found love—the fair maiden waiting for her white knight—the jaded bachelor who never believed in romance, but her incredible inertia and inexplicable energy proved him wrong. You could let yourself believe you've found something more valuable than all the money in the world; life's reset-button, a chance to start over.

The best way to sell anything is by giving it a deep and engaging origin story. *Star Wars* (1977) was a successful, standalone movie with a beginning, middle, and clearly defined end; successful enough to warrant a sequel, that George Lucas smartly spread over two additional movies. When it came time for Lucas to make even more Star Wars movies, he understood that an origin mythology *outside of the story* was just as important, if not more so, than the actual content of the story itself.

The idea that Lucas had all six Star Wars episodes written prior to making the first one gave the stories a sense of biblical grandiose, ancient texts being rediscovered. No longer was Star Wars the coming-of-age tale of a farm boy turned war hero, but the fall-and-redemption arc of Anakin Skywalker. When it came time to sell the prequels, Lucas repurposed the franchise as *the story of Darth Vader*,[42] a political drama with laser swords. The mythology eclipsed the product, infused it with a kind of historical significance, and carried the films to monetary success when the actual product being sold was a critical failure; the lie shaped our perception of the truth.

✱✱✱

But you're too far gone to let yourself believe her. If you want the real number, you'll need to speak her language; a *non-judgmental perspective*. You're hip enough to have your own crazy stories, you're on the warm side of the pool, sitting at the cool kid's table; this is the only way she'll feel comfortable telling you something more closely resembling the truth.[43] Knowing this will ruin any prospect you had of having a relationship with her—at best, you'll be another notch—and if you like her enough, you'll have wished she lied; people want you to lie.

She asked me why I write and I liked that she really wanted to know. I explained the intrinsic satisfaction of creating art; how this comes before all else, how the audience is irrelevant, how there's a purity to this approach. You'd rather have a small handful of dedicated readers invested in your work than a wider, disingenuous crowd of sycophants. She called bullshit on that. She said I write because I like attention. This is how a woman with breast implants will understand the world; feedback as the only currency that matters. You're taking time to study the rules of verse and she's rolling her eyes. You'd sooner fill a thousand marble notebooks and bury them all if they contained the right words in the right order. This is why you write; the intrinsic satisfaction of creating art. These are the lies we tell ourselves.

The lies we tell ourselves. No one fucking breaks up with me, and the ones who do will never find anyone who comes close. This was your shot and you blew it. I was too nice and you didn't appreciate it. You were only the handful of qualities I projected onto you—you have no identity beyond my perception of you—you could have been anyone, and I can replace you in a heartbeat. You were an empty vessel when we met—you were nothing—*"you were roadkill, baby, 'til I held you in my arms."*

It's better to reign in Hell than serve in Heaven. You were never the relationship type, anyway; walking through the Strawberry Festival, holding hands, in your pink polo and khakis. Big smile for the selfies she's taking for Instagram. An overpriced engagement ring to show the world that you're the sucker who thinks he finally found the right castle, and saved the right princess, when how many other assholes have there been? Big wedding with a gaudy DJ who puts wacky sunglasses on grandma. She'll hate your guts in two years. The lies we tell ourselves to justify a lifetime of nothing working out.

She told me that she likes *fuckboys,* and I thought I'd finally connected with someone; that we shared a mutual understanding of the world, that our values coalesced. That maybe a woman needs to go as far as getting plastic surgery to gain access to eternal truth; a strange condition to meet, falsify the body to free the mind. I told her that it's curious how we all prefer to be lied to. Not her, she objected—dishonesty is a big turn off, she explained—and if I wanted a date, I'd better take her to the Strawberry Festival.[44]

PURITY AND MAYHEM

"I'm breaking through, I'm bending spoons, I'm keeping flowers in full bloom; I'm looking for answers from the great beyond."

She said she wanted a fairy tale. Not something fairy tale-like or fairy tale-adjacent; not the kind they sell at Target, or the Magic Kingdom version with the anxious college girl sweating to death in her ballroom gown while telling you about all the books she read before the gnarly beast swept her away. Something where you'd never dream of compromising things with the words *good enough* to control expectations while still acknowledging the positive. She wanted the real deal.

Where it wasn't good enough to spend your nights together laughing at jokes that only you'd both understand, between bouts of incredible sex, and looking into her eyes and telling her that she was beautiful and really meaning it. This wasn't a fairy tale—this was something else—and if it wasn't good enough to be a fairy tale, what was it?

Too much of this and you're burning churches. Nothing is real until you're willing to destroy everything and sift through the ashes. Cut the throat of your father because he couldn't be what you needed.[45] Never let the lie settle; walk away from the inauthentic.

Tony Iommi didn't understand why Rob Zombie never changed out of his stage clothes; *stage clothes,* a foreign concept for Zombie, who knew you either lived your act as performance art or that it doesn't mean shit. Venom didn't understand why every Black Sabbath song wasn't about the devil; what kind of *black Sabbath* was that? Mayhem didn't think you could write dark music without making it a lifestyle and burnt churches along the Norwegian countryside; there was a purity to this.

You aren't a real writer if you consider what the reception of your writing might look like; a writer must disregard the idea of writing for an audience—there is no audience, there is only art. If you write for an audience, you may be writing words, but you aren't *making art*. Art can only manifest from the artist's subconscious, in a flow state, containing subtle and unintended nuances which even the artist may be ignorant of. This is why those who create art consider themselves conduits for God, or vessels for fairies and muses; art can only come out of the unconscious mind as a performance of self-expression. It may be cleaned up and stitched together later, but the foundation must be subconscious. If any space is surrendered to enhance the experience for an audience, you've already lost.

Black metal originated as a response to heavy metal gaining mainstream attention with artists suddenly wanting to write songs for radio airplay. Grit was lost and turned to gloss in million-dollar recording studios with smooth repeating choruses and non-threatening lyrics. Norwegian black metal artists rejected this as *inauthentic*. Heavy metal shouldn't be polished; it should conjure primal images of being alone in the woods, in late November, after midnight, with only a battery-powered cassette deck, naked and covered in animal blood…or is it your own? It should sound cold and dark.

The barrier to entry is high; Norwegian black metal is purposely abrasive. Songs cut in and out with drums loudly blasting in the foreground; there is often no discernible song structure. Vocals are sometimes used as an additional layer of sound—not its driving force—and are typically buried in the mix. Guitar riffs repeat hypnotically. They don't care if you get it or if you like it; artistic integrity devoid of concern for the audience. Kurt Cobain wishes he had their balls.

The best writing should be complex. Complicated and unrelenting. No easy reads, no bits of light fiction, nor should there be books meant to be read on the beach. Writing should challenge the reader to meet the author on his terms only. Meaning for entire pieces—entire novels—contingent on obscure references woven so seamlessly into the larger narrative that only a small percentage of readers will notice and understand. Thomas Pynchon includes a scene in *Inherent Vice* (2009) where stoner protagonist Doc Sportello charts the novel's 130 characters, and their complex relationships, on the wall of his apartment with a marker; Pynchon's way of mocking the reader. What, you can't keep up?

***

Alice lived in a house on the beach, where she hid herself away from the nasty virus. So close you could see the water from her window, in a town that seemed perpetually alive, chatter in every corner, all hours of the night. Beach houses built on the corpses of hippies, with signage proclaiming an *eternal summertime* and promises of *living easy* hanging in manicured, million-dollar love shacks. A neverending Halloween party with ghouls coming from their humble abodes, costumed as beach bums, looking for jolts from electrodes. Symbols disconnected from meaning. Only the wealthy can afford the fairy tale of pretending to be poor.

***

Her fairy tale followed a trail of breadcrumbs into the witch's oven. You only get one Weiland; everyone else is a hired gun, a studio musician, a cheap imitation. Effort can't change the immutable. When Selina Kyle tells Batman that he doesn't owe the people anything, that he's already given them *everything*, he replies, "Not everything; not yet," which is more rousing a moment for men than even the hottest pornography. Men want an excuse to give away every last bit of themselves, desperately seeking a hill to die on; a destructive purity, pure mayhem. Kill yourself finding the right castle just to save the damn princess, something Catwoman could never understand.

It wasn't the sadness in her eyes that maybe only you could see, but the way she spoke of the past; how when she said "it was a long time ago," the inflection in her voice betrayed her.

You thought you could storm in and start tearing down statues. Inexplicable confidence. Recreate the world in your own image, even if no one ever wins fighting the idealized dead. *You can't save her,* heckles Catwoman, no matter how willing you are to go down with the ship. The past has been decided, fairy tales written. Welcome to Hell; there's a purity to this.

ETERNAL SEPTEMBER

"A week without you, thought I'd forget. Two weeks without you and I still haven't gotten over you yet."

Nancy didn't like it when I teased her about her house. Put politely, it was *unfinished*. What was meant to be the baby's room, with its careful design of overlapping squares hand-painted on the walls, had become a storage space; miscellaneous items suffering a slow transition to the garbage. Her hardwood floors had stains. Light bulbs dangling from fixtures. Things in the yard that hadn't been moved since they were put down 15 years prior. A storm destroyed the fence, with only the posts a reminder that her yard had once been enclosed. The front lawn with crabgrass and mushrooms.

Not that one needed to be tremendously perceptive to realize that the house, more or less, had ceased any major evolutionary activity; the kind where the first-time homeowner is gifted a *Time-Life* "Home Repair and Improvement" book set, with plans made that foresaw holiday duties on the path to grandchildren.

She had wanted me to love the beach like she did. Reminders of this—some purchased at home furnishing stores, some given as gifts—served as the main source of décor, reminding me that the beach is her *happy place* while encouraging me to *keep calm* and *sit by the ocean*.

If there's anything certain left to believe, it's that we're living in Hell. She didn't understand why I went on about this, falling short of obsessive but with serious overtones of urgency. The greatest misconception about Hell is the fire. People think Hell is alive, molecules buzzing anxiously. There may be a cinematic quality to this, but it isn't accurate; it isn't *Hell*.

Hell is cold and dead. Hell is subtle enough for you to doubt that it's surrounding you.

I liked the beach, but I didn't love it like Nancy did. I'd meet women there for first dates, where we'd find a bench and watch the sunset as the crashing waves created an ambient soundtrack. I can't spend my days sitting on a beach; not using my time productively makes me nervous—a horrible consequence of too much time wasted—but at night, I like listening to the stories of women.

Typically divorced, but not always—the ones who were married are usually the more mentally stable—they'll cite a dead bedroom and an unmotivated husband as their chief concern for initiating the separation. There will usually be a pang of regret over disrupting the lives of their children and the inconvenience of sharing custody, although this is understood as collateral damage. They had all heard of Tinder and were "excited to try it," with the initial burst of male interest serving as enthusiastic confirmation that they made the right decision. You'll know how long a woman has been on her own by the way she talks about meeting men.

A woman new on the scene will be enamored by the attention; so many options, often exceeding her wildest fantasies. A gym rat in his early 30's looking to relieve a bit of stress after leaving the office, the 24-year-old bartender, the frat guy cheating on his teenage girlfriend; everyone vapid and interchangeable, everyone with gaudy AOL screen names, all chasing a woman over 40. She always knew she could do better than her husband, and with the maturity of age, now she's comfortable enough with her sexuality to indulge without regret.

And even if she had more fun than she ever thought was possible on those lonely nights, sitting under the glow of her television, with an open bottle of wine, playing and replaying the eventual conversation she'd need to have with her husband—even if she had gotten to live out the female version of every man's fantasy, with the only limit being a time predestined by her own genetic code, a threshold causing the attention to taper—she'll one day realize that coldness had always surrounded her, even if she couldn't always feel it.

The beach became Nancy's happy place when she found her high school sweetheart overdosed in their bathroom—dead and bloated—the beginning of her eternal September. She took their infant daughter and wouldn't return to the house for three years—the lonely princess in her decaying castle—and she did the best she could. No one could blame her for any decision she made thereafter. This is how she eased into the rest of her days, and there was nothing terribly wrong with it, even if her only wish were to politely color within the lines and walk away with a terrifically neat and tidy picture of a life well lived.

THE KING OF HELL

"Darkness will show us the way..."

Dana wouldn't let me fuck her before she went on dates. Losers she'd meet from pay-to-play dating apps, ones that supposedly offered a more serious assortment of romantic candidates. The kind she'd want to bring home to mom, assuming mom were still alive. Maybe, more accurately, the kind she'd introduce to her children; on a day trip to Adventureland, where he'd spend big money on artisan ice cream and carnival games skewed against the player.

Big smiles while riding bumper boats. This could be something real, like they advertise on TV, where aging singles find their second chance, the one that counts, as insinuated by complex smiles on the faces of couples in their forties, sipping cocoa in cozy, female-owned coffee shops; discussing *life after marriage.*

This is the one that counts. His kids are with the ex-wife, and he's booked himself an audition for a new family. He's taken her on thoughtful afternoon dates, the kind that involve pedal boats and wineries.

I wanted to fuck her before these dates, when just fucking her didn't seem like enough. I wanted my cum dripping down the inside of her thigh while she's holding hands at the Strawberry Festival. Getting laid isn't enough; you need to snort a line of ego alongside your serving of pussy. Only decadence gets you hot. You get off on chaos. You're Bob Crane on a cooking show. You want to push things until they explode.

***

Alice called me crying when she found out that her ex-husband was getting married. She didn't know where she went wrong. Let me fuck her on the first date without a condom. Girls think that's a deal breaker, that it's why they can't get a steady boyfriend, that the relinquishment of the unnatural and counterintuitive modern notion of *safe sex* signals a moral deficiency so alarming it frightens away potential mates. Make things too easy and no one sticks around.

She doesn't realize that she's in Wonderland, alone in the candy store, grabbing at tonsil ticklers with both hands. Men would kill for this experience; alone in the woods with a whittled tree branch. Covered in animal blood, or is it your own? Wit, adrenaline, and moxie; you'll need all three if you're ever getting laid again. Her ex took home the first boar he speared. Low expectations and zero confidence. The meek shall inherit the earth.

Alice didn't understand why he's getting married and she's getting fucked. I ruined her, she told me. Now she needs a man who makes her call him daddy. She's further exploring her *submissive side*. She's getting "very anal." She got a purchase confirmation for an engagement ring sent to her phone. Either their accounts are still linked, or her ex has a nasty sense of humor. Guy she's seeing calls her a fuckbuddy.

***

Lungs have felt like shit for a while now. Years of abuse. Catches up to you. Now's as good a time as any. Can work around it at the gym. Pace myself differently. Compensate with caffeine. Wit, adrenaline, and moxie. Pulmonary says its asthma; have always had it, but now it's more pronounced. Probably being polite. Too hard to explain it as a time-stamp; the remaining years are now spelled out explicitly. Timer winding down. Music intensifies, and you still haven't found the secret door out of the Forest of Illusion.

Hack garbage; too many video game references. Everything falls apart, becomes parody. Write what you know: pop culture and easy women. Married men go out on weekends with their rings in their pockets and their fingers crossed, fall asleep at night wishing they could do what you do. Wishing they were the king of shreds and patches. The King of Hell.

Handful of pills to get to sleep; not for daily use, but it's been years. Enough coffee in the morning to kill a small animal; gradually heading toward a heart attack. Kidneys are raw and irritated. Years of abuse. Right ear feels off; a warning sign. Agonizing stillness of early morning with screaming tinnitus. Too much time in headphones, at the gym, teeth-grinding black metal; but how else will you feel good enough about yourself to exude the kind of immediate confidence on first dates that you've come to get off on? Body held together with tape and glue. Push things until they explode.

***

Where were you when I was still good? Dating your high school sweetheart; college romance; first husband. Lines on the graph inching their way to the right; on the ascent. New house; 30-year mortgage. Fixed rate. We can do it, baby, us against the world. *Time-Life* "Home Repair and Improvement" book set; gut the house, make it our own. Grandchildren and holidays; a *life well lived.*

She wants her daughter to make her ashes into a gemstone. They do that now, she told me. On a necklace, passed down generationally. I'll end up in a dumpster. Possessions trashed. My death as a bit of afternoon gossip. You can be made into a tree, she told me. They do that now, she said. Maybe that will be nice?

At my best now, even with the wheels coming off. A circumstance of modernity, as unnatural as anything else. You shouldn't have gotten so many chances; game resets, save spots. You would have been killed in a war, fallen off the girder of a high-rise, hunting accident, torn apart by wolves, hanged for stupidity. You hardly deserve to have made it this far; forget soccer practice and kung-fu classes.

You were never going to be the Heartbreak Kid; you were always Cactus Jack. Spend years tearing your body apart to get to the big show, but only once you've made it do you realize that it always had to be this way. There is no winning, only consolation; scraps cobbled together. The King of Hell.

***

You need a tour rider to spend a night with a woman. Cold room for sex. If the room's too hot, show's over. Won't perform. White noise for sleeping; preferably an air filter, but a loud fan will do. I don't like "white noise machines," be it dedicated or through Alexa. I can hear where the track loops and will subconsciously internalize it, wake up every time. Need a full stock of zero-sugar late-night snacks. Need my own pillows and sleep mask. Need to pick the side of the bed. If I don't like the comforter, I'm walking. I sleep on a diagonal; this is important. The girl must compensate for this.

When they do, you realize that maybe everything has been for the sake of this moment. Maybe this wasn't your back-up plan, maybe this was by design; ass permanently kissed, demands perpetually met, ego buzzing with throbbing waves of intensity. Maybe you wanted desperate women looking to you as their last chance.

Wait long enough and their line on the graph drops low enough for you to be their savior. The king of terrified women. Terrified of aging, of smile lines and crow's feet, of sagging breasts and tight jeans. Terrified of being alone. The King of Hell.

***

Dana did all the right things this time around. She went through a phase where she'd have men from hookup dating apps meet at her house; a kind of post-divorce mania. She'd be drinking, of course; she couldn't meet strangers for sex otherwise.

Not this time, she told me. She wanted to take things slowly; go on real dates, pedal boats and wineries. The Strawberry Festival. Long conversations in female-owned coffee shops about travel. This was how to get a boyfriend. This was how to fall in love.

And once enough flowers were gifted, enough day trips to the country were taken; walks in the park and train station county fairs. Once there was enough for it not to seem cheap, she had him over for sex. Text the next day, like clockwork, likely prewritten, copied and pasted; he doesn't feel a strong enough connection. They don't have the kind of chemistry he's looking for. He wishes her luck.

He knew what was needed to get sex; money to spend, expectations to meet. He's NASA developing the astronaut pen because he doesn't have the balls to be a Soviet, alone with a pencil.[46] Cost of doing business. Rats on a sinking ship, grabbing at what we can, both hands, blood everywhere. She learned her lesson this time, she tells me. Come by and fuck me early, she texts. She had a date that night.

SET IT AND FORGET IT

"Row like a felon, drown like a captain's son. But say, how long can this go on?"

The goal is a clear stretch of highway long enough to keep your cruise control set at 78. Detach from the minutia of traffic while feeling connected to the reality of the journey; wheels groping pavement, cutting through morning air. Not only does your attention to speed management ultimately save on gas mileage, but more importantly, it provides space to sharpen the mind/body connection that's crucial for when you walk into work at 6AM—each motion light clicking to life as you pass—to sit at your desk and write in a spiral-bound notebook for 25 minutes before starting your work for the day.

Cafeteria duty has become dedicated to reading and tuning out coworker chatter about meals past and upcoming; Steve pursuing the perfect combination of pizza toppings, Larry the Security Guard having meatloaf again but it's okay because *Larry loves meatloaf*. You can't ask them to stop talking, but you'd like to, even if only to emphasize the importance of finding time to read every day.

Reading is like the leg day of writing: it's easy to skip a few times and then walk away altogether thinking you don't really need it, which is when your writing turns to shit. You could read things you enjoy, but you're better off finding something that helps organize your thoughts into stronger prose; if what you're reading doesn't strengthen your voice as a writer, sorry, bucko, put the comic book down and find something better suited to maximize productivity. Idiot thought reading was supposed to be enjoyable?

Lunch isn't about eating lunch; actually eating lunch is for suckers.

People with their lavish, restaurant-style meals; plates getting heated in microwaves, an army of Tupperware coming out of satchels, menus and take-out. You don't need any of this—you need a pen and a printed copy of what will be your first book; reading print and editing by hand has a different feel than sitting in front of a desktop—a different perspective. Both necessary to end up with a product that will make sense of an otherwise wasted 40 years. There is nothing more important than this.

You try to get all of your actual work—the work you get paid for, the work you disregard as bullshit—done in one shot. You've front-loaded your school year with large, time-consuming projects so you can spend the rest of your time writing; work you will never get paid for, work you consider with dire importance. Writing gives you a sense of relief when feeling anxious—purpose when feeling like you've ruined your life and wasted your time—meaning when thinking about the meaningless of your death.

***

I killed my teacher, my kid girlfriend had told me. She was excited. Her math teacher died after sending her father an email about how disappointed she was in the kid's lack of participation in class; supposedly she died, like, within an hour of sending the email. Last thing she did. Maybe the last thing she thought about. Class participation. A funny story for the kid to tell people. No one cares and you'll end up in a dumpster with some asshole laughing at you. This is your life.

***

After work, you rush home to get your gym gear on. You've settled on a two-days-on-one-day-off-three days-on-two-days-off lifting schedule, with your days set at chest and shoulders, legs and abs, back and arms. You learned the virtue of rest days during quarantine. You also learned that a weighted vest maximizes your time spent walking after the gym, which is anywhere between four-and-a-half to ten miles per day.

Dinner is your one meal per day, and is usually some combination of steak, eggs, pork, and chicken. You feel guilty indulging in Quest cookies before bed, which have become the bane of your weekday existence but also what you most look forward to; the gift and the curse, the sacred and the profane. You spend a lot of time thinking about processed, low-sugar protein cookies. This is your life.

Don't message me for fitness advice, because now you know everything I know. That's the only way I know how to do it. I only know the hard way, every time. I've been fat; women treat you like a leering retard and people at work talk down to you. I'd rather drop dead from my awful schedule than deal with another second of that ever again.

***

You actually tell people you go to bed at 8 o'clock, a coworker enquired. Earnestly. She thought this made me look crazy, that I don't spend my time watching streaming television shows that remind people of the inherent badass nature of white suburban women, drinking wine, enjoying my time in a kind of free-floating, unscheduled manner. Unproductive. Repulsive. Enjoy your time off the work farm, plebs; I'll be here grinding myself to death.

I have nothing in common with people who don't understand the urgency of getting to bed early—sleeping away my two hours at the gym, ten miles walking with 20 pounds on my back, the 3,000 calories of meat—sleep substituting for meditation, dreaming productively, waking up with total mental clarity and peak creative energy. Racing to work to write in a fucking notebook; the most important thing you do, what must be guarded before all else. Avoiding morning greetings and polite chit-chat from well-meaning coworkers; vicious mind-erasers and psychic vampires, all of them. Everything in service of writing in the fucking notebook because writing in the notebook is all you fucking have.

***

This is a test from God, he said to himself. He wrote this on his Internet weblog. Autocorrect, always sure to capitalize the "i" in Internet but never the "g" in God. He tried to feel the presence of God in his daily life, but he settled on the idea that it would be better if he didn't. Faith is a test of your mettle. Better that He stay hidden. I can take it, he thought. Meaning, slipping through his fingers like sand. Body falling apart. Watching his parents die. I can take it, he thought.

Grinding away, expecting something to click, to make sense, just once. Stay hidden; God-faith is having belief despite insurmountable energy urging toward disbelief. Faith is a challenge; faith is a choice. Easy to believe when everything is handed to you; money, women, meaning. Don't make sense of this for me, God, I can take it, I can do better; I can start getting to bed at 7:45.

YOU'RE JUST LIKE DELICIOUS TACOS

"Whoever thought you'd be better at turning a screw than me? I do it for my life. Fuck yeah!"

You're just like Delicious Tacos, he told me. He was messaging me for advice. Girl problems, but more than that too, he said. His life felt empty. He was lacking direction; depression, anxiety. There's something about my writing that suggests I could offer intervention; a quick series of bullet points or if/then statements. Something about my writing that's aspirational.

I'm willing to believe this. Despite my failures, which I've grown comfortable sharing with strangers, I'm a happy and centered person. I have positive habits, and even if my addictive personality will merely cut and paste beneficial habits in place of those destructive and pursue them with the same psychotic vigor, they're at least theoretically contributing to my overall health and well-being.[47] I read and write regularly. I lift weights and take long walks. I meditate and enjoy stillness. I love nature. I believe in God.

I'm just like Delicious Tacos. I write about getting laid, as a single man, in realistic terms. No big fish stories; the raw honesty of average women. This lends me credibility with those hard-up enough to find something like that impressive. Scarier are the types who take jabs and call it "fan fiction." Sex alone has become the big fish story, with the same anxious energy of when you would've killed a small animal to see tits as a 13-year old; relentless and aching.

They all want *Magic's Biggest Secrets Finally Revealed* (1997). As if the plethora of Internet content describing it in detail has become too slick, too Hollywood, just as detached from reality. Average men spend a lifetime studying bullshit to screw a fraction of what the dirtbag bartender is pulling strung out. The quickest way to cut the line is a bag of cocaine. I know this because Delicious Tacos knows this.

Stay single long enough with your eyes open, talk to enough women, and you're going to come to the same conclusions. Once more men get it, society will fall. The trick is to have your interests align with what women find attractive; interests so personally fulfilling that if you never get laid again, they become spiritual quests. Without sex, lifting weights takes on a more authentic gravitas. The creation of good art—good as defined by your own standard—will mean more than any woman's opinion of you. A deep connection to nature. Reflections on philosophy, history, and morality. The ability to make yourself laugh. Good food. Presence. This is the advice I would give; or just get a bag of cocaine.

You're not like Delicious Tacos, Blair told me. I had lent her *Savage Spear of the Unicorn* (2020); I wanted to hear her thoughts on what I consider *true contemporary literature*. She has a masters from an Ivy League university, she reads Pynchon, she tells me I'm great. She's smart. She liked Tacos, but she doesn't see the similarities, and maybe I don't either. Tacos is taller with a full head of hair, in better shape despite us both spending years at the gym, 20,000 Twitter followers, multiple books and fucks more women, even if he's paying for some of them.

I aspire to be Delicious Tacos, in a one-sided competition, existing solely in my own head. I'm Dave Mustaine to his Metallica, and maybe *Rust in Peace* (1990) is the technically superior heavy metal record, taking thrash to its logical conclusion. Maybe the Megadeth listener is the more sophisticated music fan, sipping chardonnay and discussing the subtle intricacies of Dave's deep-in-the-mix guitar fills. Pointing out how *Youthanasia* (1994) was recorded completely live in the studio as a *fuck you* to Metallica's partial live recording of the *Black Album*—a fact that was presumably only for Mustaine's own mental satisfaction—that he's better than Metallica.

Even when the hard reality of metrics—sales figures and tickets sold—don't agree. That Dave can be a better lead guitar than Kirk, a better songwriter than Hetfield/Ulrich, a better leading man than James; at least in his own head, where he can set the parameters and claim victory. You're not like Delicious Tacos, baby; lending her books with a gun to her head. You're better; *it should be you*.[48]

Online content is mostly bullshit. The impulse is to fill dead air. If enough empty space elapses, you end up firing whatever you have in the chamber—sound and fury, signifying nothing—into cyberspace like a drunk frat boy feeding quarters into a *Space Invaders* (1978) cabinet at a dusky college bar in 1982; haphazard shots fired into the night sky, just hoping to hit something. Just like what I'm doing right now—earn credibility with literary references; paint a fuzzy picture of video game nostalgia—people like that. Write about someone more popular than yourself; maybe the uninitiated will be baited to click? Maybe Tacos will re-Tweet? Maybe he'll be flattered and say, "That Bad Billy: not so bad after all!"

I told him to find peace within himself. Partake in things he enjoys. Realize his passion and pursue it with psychotic vigor. Consider himself dead, right now, and think about what he would've liked to have left behind; now, work backwards, and find a way to achieve it. This is all that matters.

You get enough sex and you realize that the girls you jerk off to are wispy fantasies, something that reality will hardly ever match. The percentage of truly great sex you end up having is so miniscule that it should be disregarded on its face—living for the weekend, teachers obsessed with the school calendar—focus on sex and you'll never stop missing your life. Thanks, he told me. He'll think about it, he said. And in the meantime, he'll shoot Delicious Tacos another DM; maybe this time, Tacos will write back.

GHOSTBUSTERS 2

"The ghosts that roam this house, like winter air right through our souls..."

You don't have to write about my stairs, she said, and we can only be friends if you stop hurting my feelings. I didn't have to be in the room to know what Nancy's eyes would have looked like—desperate to hide the depth of her vulnerability—but like every other time, no matter how hard she tried, the way she looked at you betrayed her. This was what made you fall in love with her. She stopped talking to you when you posted the piece about her house—her house as a metaphor for every bit of hurt, every battle scar, every coping strategy and defense mechanism; walls and coldness—circles that needed squaring. Parts of her life to be compartmentalized; some locked away, some delicately framed with self-talk.

It was a long time ago, she'd tell me; with just enough hesitation, half-seconds further halved, moments so brief that you were certain you were the only one to ever notice, like Meriwether Lewis crisscrossing the uncharted West. New territory to discover and examine and critique. To write about; a loving tribute, as if to say: I see who you really are and I want to use every bit of energy I have to protect that.

She didn't see it that way; over the course of our time together, but also in the piece about her house. Like tricking Rocky Balboa into being on a news bit meant to humiliate him, she saw it as a *cheap shot*. Come laugh at the sweet, entirely normal woman—who never wanted to be written about, used as fodder for Internet web clicks—the entirely normal woman, who takes comfort in the "My Heart is at the Beach" throw-pillow; the entirely normal woman, with the dead husband and the unfinished house, who never felt she had anything to prove to anyone, and now you want to rub her face in it.

And even if you explained that it was meant to make her seem sympathetic in the face of awful people who make awful decisions, this was sympathy she never asked for.

***

It's funny, but it's not a joke, Blair explained to me. I have a difficult time with this distinction. Blair's good for things like that; smart, Ivy League whatever, IQ likely a standard deviation above average. I think you're *emotionally abusive,* she told me. She sent an infographic explaining the qualities of a *manipulative narcissist;* red flags, she told me, with the wide eyes of sincerity.

It's not funny, she insisted. I told her that I'd cut-and-paste the list to my OkCupid profile. OkCupid, because anyone who hasn't already switched to Bumble is expecting a little abuse. You're doing it again, she told me; this is emotional abuse.

And maybe she was right; it read like a personality description of someone awful enough to be me. I never shy away from conflict, especially when I'm "fighting to be right." I try to get women to think *exactly like me,* and will not accept *conflicting narratives.* I often tell women that they love me and ask them to repeat it. I prefer when a woman mirrors my emotions; if I'm laughing, I didn't hurt your feelings, it was just teasing, you big baby, and you should be laughing, too. In this regard, I will deny someone's experiences if I don't agree with their emotional reaction, using phraseology like "it wasn't that bad."

I always prefer women to read my mind, mood, or body language; my mood which will shift, erratically and arbitrarily, throughout the day. I talk about myself incessantly—I have a fucking blog where I expect strangers to be fascinated with me—I am self-obsessed. In this regard, I am always sure my needs are being met before *checking in on her.*

I'm insensitive, I told her. It's my worst quality. Please try to be understanding.

***

You can write about my stairs if you don't use the picture I sent you, she told me. I don't do well with if/then statements. I can't be told what to do; natural inertia forcing decisions to be made in the opposite direction, even to my own detriment. I couldn't understand why she didn't just sell the house, anyway. The past died on its own, no killing required; board up the old place and forget about it. She had the market on her side, riding the tide of an inflating bubble; photogenic good looks. Burn the boats on your way to a second life.

I have to use the picture of your actual stairs, I explained to her. For purposes of authenticity. Like the most damaged egomaniacs of my generation, I'm obsessed with authenticity. Every bit of output—words written, social interactions had, emotions expressed—must be organically sensed with a blind, Jedi-like intuition. I am not someone who enjoys small-talk; pitiful social grooming for the less intelligent. I like to discuss *ideas*. Everything I've written about—personal lives dissected, women scolded for making what is quite clearly the wrong decision in retrospect— is exactly how it happened; at least, certainly, a close approximation. From my own perspective; from the godly throne at my computer.

She stopped talking to you when you posted the piece about her house, and you thought she was being a big baby. She said her feelings were hurt, but you thought she just wanted to get her way, that she was being manipulative. Exert a little bit of power; have you take your piece down; she always made snide comments about your writing. Started seeing her again during the summer—had broken up right before quarantine; it felt like ages had passed but also no time at all. Was already seeing other women, and you wanted her to know. No one fucking breaks up with me. Now was your time to rub her face in it.

I started working on my house, she told me. She was proud of the changes she made; home improvement, they call it, and she did it all on her own. But it was when you got the picture of her freshly-stained stairs that it hit you; so hard that you needed a minute to compose yourself. She was doing all this because of what you wrote. She cares about what you think. You made her feel embarrassed; ashamed. You hurt her feelings.

Stay alone long enough, you learn to only trust yourself, not other people; their motives seem disingenuous. They are inauthentic, unlike you. Perfect son of God; purity of heart, purity of intention.

A writer; an artist; this must come before all else, at the expense of feelings being hurt, relationships damaged beyond repair. This is what you tell yourself to get to sleep at night; still necessary even after the handful of pills. This is what you tell yourself when you know you're just a selfish asshole, a parody of a human being, a bad sequel. The King of Hell, on your throne at your computer.

I have to use the picture of your stairs, I told her—I'm a writer, I'm an artist, I'm an asshole—anything else, of course, would be inauthentic.

JENNIFER LOST THE WAR

"...but will the morning headlines even say that it's a shame?"

They're all liars, she told me, all of them. While we had spoken a few times, only through text, in the years since things had come apart violently, I finally chipped away at Jennifer enough for a phone call. Years had passed, and maybe the resulting body image issues—collateral damage from getting off on calling her fat—had faded enough for the sound of my voice to be somewhat less nauseating. Or maybe it was the *mid-August blues;* five months into quarantine and just about any option seems great—a fact that I greatly benefitted from over the summer—but even if I had been excited to catch up with Jennifer formally, this wasn't what I was expecting.

It was only a few years prior, the summer of 2018, where she had told me to "fuck off" on account of how she could "fuck anyone she wanted" and wouldn't consider wasting her time "fucking me," a point I half-heartedly attempted contesting but would ultimately concede. If I could *fuck anyone,* I wouldn't be spending time doing any of this shit; dear reader, you'd be the one "fucking off."

But, luckily for us all, I need this and I need you—*desperately*—so here we are together. I never flew too close to the sun because I never had the option; eternally shackled to Hell's version of Marley's chains: the curse of the average man. But the average single woman in her thirties won't feel the swirled cocktail of *gift and curse* that sexual restrictions bring and will typically indulge in ways that'd make her bright-eyed 24-year-old self blush like she's at Plato's Retreat.

Jennifer was at the end of this ride—spent all her tickets on the log flume at Adventureland, and even if she had a great time, now she had to sit in her wet jeans on the ride home—they're *all liars*.

The election didn't come up this time around. Four years prior, it may as well have been foreplay. Deliberate triggering and antagonization. The last time a presidential election will feel significant, subversive, defining. What we had before us was space to make our own. Space for like-minded people to feel less lonely, less disconnected. There were people like us all around, quietly noticing things about the broken modern world; buzz like a Bethesda message board on the first day of release. Coming together and creating energy that was impossible to ignore; madness in every direction: blogs and memes, even better than our *wildest dreams*. A decentralized, meritocratic culture war was one we could win. This was our time and we weren't going to let it get away. Our time, where fucking Jennifer while wearing a Trump hat felt significant, subversive, and defining.

There was a definite thrill to having sex in a Trump hat, of conquering and winning. Part of the energy wave that we created together, each contributing a fraction of a fraction until it took on its own electromagnetic momentum, one that we were able to tap into on the back end like a perpetual motion machine; bumps of highly potent, 140-character at-a-time good shit.

We had won the election, we beat the establishment; David kicking Goliath in the balls, Little Mac knocking Super Macho Man the fuck out. We were all Ricky Vaughn and Ricky Vaughn was emblematic of us all. We could fuck anyone we wanted, at least spiritually, symbolically.

The crest of a high and beautiful wave.

They're all liars is probably what she wasn't expecting, but like the song quote Ellis used to set up *Less Than Zero* (1985), "this is the game that moves as you play," and more often than not, faster than you're able to notice. While she's screwing Mr. Exciting—the guy she knows will never commit—she's betting the house on the idea that those who are *less exciting* will be there for her when she's done sowing the last bits of her post-divorce *wild oats*. The real shock hits when Mr. Dependable starts playing games too, and the only way he knows how—the long con—pedal boats and wineries, boring, limp-dick sex that she has to grit her teeth through just to say she has a boyfriend—and then he treats her like shit all the same.

The election didn't come up this time with Jennifer because the energy had already dissipated. The game's been rigged with the conclusion foregone; this wasn't what we were expecting. Biden will stand as a puppet for the neoliberal world order; Ricky Vaughn in handcuffs. This was the end of the beginning; a comfort to Jennifer who was someone outside of Internet culture, who liked Marvel movies and sharing memes about Mondays, who had thought that as long as there was a woman present in places where decisions were being made, all was right in the world. That as long as we send the orange man packing, we can resume a life of corporate-approved consumer experiences—and with our pictures on all the requisite dating apps, we can become the product—for all the liars to consume.

ONLY DEATH IS REAL

"...beneath the sound of hope."

It's the same thing every time, she told me. It's an act, the whole thing; it isn't real. The eye contact, the pursed lips, hands in the hair, the inflection in tone: "baby, baby…" She'll pick up on this and mimic it back to me; same eye contact, same pursed lips: "baby, baby…"

When you've lived what feels like a thousand lifetimes compared to the high school sweethearts, you've figured out every bit of the female algorithm; missile launch codes carved into your skull like the password to skip to Mike Tyson; right to the bedroom, right to true love, scientific discovery at the price of normalcy; at the price of family.

At the price of outliving your parents, at least numerically. Without anything else—anything to provide perspective—the single man will either self-destruct in addiction or grind himself into the ground; defiance on the road to decay, defiance in the face of genetic limitations, trying to get muscle car performance out of an economy class. Your parents were shopping on a budget; who knew how bad things would get?

***

The cold void of an endless January seems even crueler when juxtaposed with the colored lights of December. It was a December morning, before first period, that our eyes met in front of her locker. In what couldn't have been planned, at least consciously planned—perhaps more like the march of the penguins, or a rosebud uncoiling before the relentless morning sun—perhaps something guided by nature and etched into a plan that wasn't within our power to modify. Our eyes met, guided by invisible forces so strong that they had almost revealed themselves—a proof for God, had we been more conscious of it in the moment—our eyes met and hung in the air frozen. No words exchanged. Even a kiss would have spoiled the purity of the moment. We had from our surroundings what was needed, and we could make from it something more.

We stayed after school that day and spent the afternoon talking about the future as if we could write it. Too shy, of course, to include one another in these plans, but we spoke in ways where this acknowledgement wasn't necessary; that it was maybe so pressing and obvious that it could be left unsaid.

That night, December 16th, 1996, I took the late bus home from school, and that night was the only time I wore a seatbelt. This was the greatest day of my life, and I couldn't let anything ruin it.

***

You're just like Stanley Kubrick is what people must have told Shane Carruth. Absolute darling of the independent movie scene at the dawn of the new millennium, Carruth did what would have been considered impossible: made his first movie, with a $7,000 budget, and won the grand-jury prize at Sundance. To put this in perspective, it's like your friend's student film winning an Oscar; like breaking a law of nature, this was something that *couldn't happen*...but it did, because *Primer* (2004) is incredible. Breathtakingly incredible—even with its flaws; flubbed audio and blown-out lighting—there is nothing like *Primer* and *Primer* is fucking incredible.

And even still, I can never decide whether I prefer Primer or Carruth's follow-up *Upstream Color* (2013), a film so uniquely outside the box that I wouldn't know where to begin describing it. Part science fiction, part cold realism—broken people with interdependent relationships—*Upstream Color* examines the connection between identity and trauma, how the latter inescapably shapes the former—and, more so, how these elements, so crucial to how we understand the world around us, are often invisible.

Absolute darling of the independent movie scene, for a short time, Carruth had tried to work within the Hollywood system, to the point of even pitching a Batman movie. When he couldn't get funding for his big budget, trippy sci-fi adventure *A Topiary*, he pivoted back to realism with *A Modern Ocean,* which caught a bit of fire, even making it to the casting stage…and then nothing.

Absolute darling of the independent movie scene, which is ultimately meaningless. No one wants to finance difficult, obtuse art. No one cares how good you are. No one cares if you're just like Stanley Kubrick, or just like Delicious Tacos, your inaccessible art—your brilliance—means nothing in a world of Mickey Mouse superhero bullshit. Beauty means nothing in Hell.

***

It was in the cold void of January that Kevin had slipped you the little blue sheet of paper, folded up with your name across the front, during second-period Theology. You had nothing to worry about, he said. He wasn't interested, he explained. He was already dating Michelle; a fact you all knew, but Jessica had still called him the night before just to be sure.

It is only in the cold void of an endless January that all can be laid bare. Only in the absence of the ornate, and the emotions inherently consequent, that proper assessment can be made. Only after New Year's Eve, 1996; making out with Jessica in her living room; Dick Clark with KISS ringing in the New Year; "I wanna rock and roll all nite and party *every day*"; drunk only on each other; hands in her hair, looking into her eyes—this is gonna be our year, baby—only in the absence of this can things be properly contextualized.

Terms and conditions; hypothesis and conclusion; the manager who won't let the artist pursue their passion project for practical reasons. Hollywood who won't give Shane Carruth money to make pure art. She was the prize and you were the runner-up; second choice. She tried to negotiate for a better deal but chose to accept the offer on the table. You bought what you could afford and were happy with what you got. One little blue sheet of paper later and it was tainted, like finding a horde of ants behind the wall of your dream house or the new car that never leaves the shop. A heap of junk who'd tell you that she loved you but you weren't buying it—it wasn't *good enough*—who cried at your coldness and sucked your dick on Friday night. You wanted a fairy tale; you wanted purity and you got mayhem.

The punchline is that Jessica loved me for years after we broke up. For years, she'd do her best to find me; in the years before social media, this wasn't easy. Messages sent through friends. Showing up at the same goth clubs. *Desperately Seeking Susan* (1985); always a step behind, always on the prowl. She'd let a guy hit on her and I'd swoop in and pull her away by the waist.

No one could understand why I wouldn't just date her. If you saw the dress she'd wear to Detour, you'd have wondered the same thing, but she just had the dumb luck of knowing me. She had the dumb luck of buying all those Seattle stocks at their IPO, the dumb luck of buying Bitcoin for pennies, an *early adopter;* commendable, but now she could step aside 'cause this rocket's not stopping 'til we hit the moon. Thanks for playing, baby. Maybe next time.

***

Writing is the pursuit of truth; this is what you'll say when asked why you write. Greatness existing within your reach; brief glimpses of its Platonic form, so brief you can only sketch them from memory; scribble out words, inadequate substitutions for what you're trying to impale with your ballpoint spear; feel the juices stream down your neck as you indulge on the progress you've made. The pursuit of truth; there's a purity to this.

Internet fame, a substitute for your relationship with God. This is what you say matters. This is how you get to sleep at night. This is how you justify a meandering existence, never having to commit, always thinking you could do better; you *should* do better. Incredible truth to be found in meeting desperate women on dating apps. There's no room in Hell for the happily married; only the dead walk the Earth.

As if David Foster Wallace's suicide doesn't haunt you. Poke holes in your theory. You'll never be as good—you'll never be as acclaimed, historically significant, critically well-received, famous—both Internet and *real life*. Even this, what you woke up early to write, before work, in a spiral-bound notebook that you bought for a quarter; even this, your recent work—which you believe shows significant growth; your stylistic prime; your best, which by anyone's judgement would have to be considered clever—will always be shit compared to Wallace's worst…and even if you want to believe that turning words into art is enough to justify an otherwise meaningless existence, DFW's hanging corpse is somewhere laughing at you.

AFTER HOURS

"If you close the door, the night could last forever..."

It's okay to do nice things, Blair explained. She had made a reservation for the afternoon at a winery operating on a working beef farm. Anything pretentious would be tempered by a kind of rustic authenticity. They'll have cows, she told me.

Although it can be managed, it's impossible to entirely diminish feelings of hesitancy in a struggle that I can only assume is similar to the misnomer of the *recovering drug addict*—the same wishful thinking involved—that one can ever, successfully, erase the footprint; bust the ghost…thoughts wander; compulsions linger restlessly. There is no recovery for true addiction.

You've been around too long to think it's a good idea. You've seen too much. Instincts adopted and ingrained, that trigger semi-automatically; the lunging of the rattlesnake; fight or flight, and most times it's a combination of the two. Survival: running for your life from Blinky and Clyde, always looking for your next power pellet to turn the tables and devour them all. Quick and bloodless. Get them before they get you.

Just be normal, okay? Bright eyes pleading with the urgency of a death row inmate waiting on a morning execution. You can tell a lot by the way a woman looks at you; her wants and needs, the vulnerabilities she thinks she's hiding. She thought she was lucky to meet you and you seem intent on proving her wrong.

Just be normal. Holding hands at the Strawberry Festival doesn't signal weakness; that you're easy prey, that you're entirely unlike the guy who'd treat her like shit. The one she'd idolize; that even in Hell, sometimes you can sit back and turn your brain off, like you're watching the Incredible Hulk save a busload of trans kids from right-wing terrorists. You can forget what you know and enjoy the moment. Holding hands while tasting an eclectic variety of artisan wines. It's okay to do nice things.

Blair bought me a gratitude journal for Christmas. It's best to focus on the positive, she explained. Careful to read every word I write and tell me that I'm great, even when I don't see it. Blair likes to make me feel good about myself. She's thoughtful like that. Her biggest concern is whether I'll like the pot roast on a Saturday night. I've never made one before, she'll remind me.

As if I'd know the difference; living like a ghoul for so long, you lose sight of these things. Meals with more than one ingredient. Showers without mold in the grout. Toilet seats attached to their namesake. The *little things,* which Blair has perfected.

Our waitress is a pretty, salt-of-the-earth ginger. The type of girl who doesn't exist in any location where she'd actually be able to be your girlfriend. The mask she's wearing engenders the fantasy that she's a doppelganger for every ginger you've ever wanted; the *fuckin' D-girl* that Chrissy gets a taste of in season two of *The Sopranos* (2000), a scene which you carefully utilized what was then emerging technology—the clarity and frame-by-frame precision of digital video—to jack off to the glimpse of her breasts when gifted the season box set 20 years prior.

She takes you into the meat freezer and apologizes that organ meat is temporarily unavailable; an experimental recipe she's working on. This is how she spends her weekends, she says, embarrassed. I feel no obvious chemistry between us, but I wonder. What would be the right words to say? The right order? Nintendo passwords and missile launch codes. How would you open?

***

I wonder what it would have been like if we knew each other as college freshmen, Blair said aloud—not exactly as a question that necessarily required an answer; not a genuine inquiry, but rather wistful romanticism, meant to hang in the air as the opposite of a tragic *missed opportunity*—an adorable *what if.* I told her that we wouldn't have known each other, her as a hopeful sorority pledge—sure of nothing but enjoyable experiences on the horizon for the next decade, a certainty she'd bet the house on—and me in my black jeans and Misfits T-shirt, smoking clove cigarettes around the time I realized that life only gets a little bit worse with each passing year. Explaining to Blair that women *exist* and men are *made;* that women are gifted their value *up front,* that as a college freshman she was living a lifestyle equivalent to that of a millionaire playboy at a beach resort; the world at her knees, only good vibes on the agenda. She wouldn't be caught dead talking to a ghoul whose invite to the party must've gotten lost in the mail.

So why cash out now? Finally clawed my way into what's left; mostly empties and spilled beer. Vomit caked into the carpet, stinking of acid and sulfur. Why settle now that I can revel in the shit heap—the King of Hell—aging women at my knees, like the cover of *Love Gun* (1977). My line on the graph infinitely heading toward the top; with another month at the gym, 10,000 Twitter followers, a million-dollar Bitcoin; I'll get there eventually. Why should I settle—the God of thunder, taking what's left and using every last bit—the Ed Gein of dating. You don't cash your chips in ten minutes after learning to count cards, but how much blood needs to be spilled, Vlad?

Revolt against the modern world or revel in its destruction? You feel owed this for every bit of shit you had to eat. For every disappointment you've suffered, for the promises broken, for the deliberate subterfuge in the form of memes embedded in a pop culture that you still consider warm and nostalgic; you're the institutionalized prisoner, the slave finding comfort in his chains, Patty Hearst with a machine gun. So far off-course, buried under relentless waves, carried out to nowhere. You were wronged by a world encouraging exploration and experience, and now that you finally got your ticket punched and your hiking boots on, you're not turning the ship around and heading home. Every day is Halloween and you're going as a coked-up sorority girl—Tyler Hadley with a hammer— you're going to push things until they explode. You're a fucking rock star, with your sideways cap and reasonably ageless face, and if they try to throw you out now, you'll kill to party. This is what you wanted, and you'll get what you deserve. Just be normal, okay? Welcome to fucking Hell.[49]

ENDNOTES

[1] Zenith television sets manufactured before 1990 had a quirk so pervasive that considering it a manufacturer's defect might seem unfair to those who try harder to put out quality products: a loud buzzing sound emitted when the screen was blank. If you had a Zenith set at the time, you'd have assumed this noise was part of the program you were watching. So when the screen fades to black after a dramatic cliffhanger ending to the first part of a very special episode edition of a sitcom, you'd have assumed the jarring buzz was meant for dramatic effect.

[2] Henry Frankenstein because I love the movie and don't care about the book. I have tremendous fondness for the Universal Monster movies, and Colin Clive's portrayal of the mad scientist is absolutely iconic; even more so, as Clive died only a few years after making *The Bride of Frankenstein* (1935) and was probably drunk while shooting both.

[3] KISS is the only rock band primarily operating in the genre of *success*. While their first few albums flailed wildly due to an artistic innocence met with a lack of precedent and heavy guesswork—resulting in a reliance on authenticity, a creative process that must have nauseated Gene Simmons—once KISS figured out what KISS should be, they put out two albums of KISS music in its purest form (*Rock and Roll Over* [1976] and *Love Gun* [1977]), albums I would recommend for those asking, "what is KISS?" However, as a group pioneering the *genre of success*, growth potential is an idea that must be discussed and revisited with regularity. Like any niche form of entertainment, KISS assumed their core audience was a constant, something to be taken for granted and abused,[a] and concentrated their focus on capturing mainstream attention. Which resulted in a disco-

tinged hit single, a bubblegum pop album, a Star Wars-inspired concept album, hair metal, attempts at *serious heavy metal* when it was situationally appropriate, a forgotten grunge record, and, finally, exploitative nostalgia targeted at the core audience they wanted to financially drain, but with enough historic cache to attract the bored boomer looking for a few hours of 1970's good vibes on a Saturday night.

    a. In fairness to Simmons and Stanley, they were right; inherent to being a member of the KISS Army is having a fetish for financial domination.

[4] I got to see my dog in a dream the other night. I am grateful for that. I hope to see him again someday.

[5] The expectation of having a remarkable life; one of the worst bits of irreversible collateral damage of the Hollywood system.

[6] Not only has Hollywood promised a remarkable life, but the pervasive nature of media has framed our memories in ways that fit narrative archetypes. People will frame past relationships—their formation and dissolution—in dramatic terms that are most likely contrived; attraction, and its subsequent decay, isn't terribly complex or interesting. However, Hollywood has provided a tool kit to make these things sound glamorous and tragic. To what degree of how we remember our own lives, nostalgia and the idealized past—our own memories—will have been tampered with by the media we've consumed over the years?

[7] "Those other girls aren't real."

    Christine went to great lengths to convince someone that she wasn't like *those other girls.* Her experiences had greater depth, her thoughts were more developed, her interests were more artistic, and her feelings were more genuine. Christine had esoteric qualities that made her *special* and *unique*, while those other girls were basic and shallow. Christine also had a bigger waist and fatter thighs.

    She wasn't fat, but Christine was conscious of her limitations and adjusted accordingly. If she couldn't compete with *those other girls,* Christine would attempt to redefine what it meant to be attractive and then try to convince men that what they thought they wanted was all wrong.

The blonde cheerleader with the big chest wasn't cool like Christine. She didn't like indie music nor artsy movies, she didn't read interesting novels, she didn't have an ironic taste in fashion, nor would she be happy having a night in drinking beers and playing *Mario Kart*. She wasn't *real*, and Christine was; real is what you should want.

Christine thought she needed to leverage authenticity, in the form of a meticulously sculpted identity, to compensate for not being as aesthetically competitive. Christine believed that with enough salesmanship and authenticity, she could land a rock star boyfriend.

When people aren't aesthetically gifted enough to organically attract those whom they feel entitled to dating, they attempt to change the parameters of attraction through trickery and sophistry. They redefine attraction and attempt to sell the redefinition.[a]

    a.   To Kill a Mockingbird (1960).

[8] *Over the Edge* (1979).

[9] Casey Anthony epitomized something that I couldn't quite put my finger on as I sat on my couch, eating Captain Crunch and smoking weed, watching the coverage of her trial during a tranquil evening in the summer of 2011.

There was something missing from my life at the time…I wasn't conscious of it, but felt its weight all the same. It wasn't that I was unhappy. I was definitely comfortable; I had a career made possible through the empty achievement of multiple college degrees, I had a fat girlfriend who was a *crazy bitch* but I *loved her anyway*, and I spent my free time feeling good…after all, life was about maximizing consumption while sleepwalking through minimal responsibility. The idea of ambition beyond this baseline was something foreign and laughable. Isn't that the American dream?

Yet still…alternating between video games, television, pornography, processed food, oxytocin, and marijuana left a fuzzy feeling on my brain that something wasn't quite right, but I wasn't quite ready to see it just yet…

Casey's story would never have worked as a piece of fiction; it wouldn't have been believable. A pretty brunette gets knocked up by a stranger on the Florida house party circuit and decides to keep the baby...and ends up missing the party lifestyle so much that she murders her own two-and-a-half-year-old daughter to hit up the party scene harder than before. A true story of dopamine addiction gone mad.

And, as if to drive things into the realm of the surreal, push things until they explode, in the month before her arrest, she was so thrilled to have thought that she had gotten away with murder that she got a tattoo to commemorate the occasion ("Bella Vita").

Casey couldn't give up the college girl lifestyle of enjoyable experiences and good vibes. She killed to party.

The media coverage would have tried to convince you that Casey was an anomaly worthy of social crucifixion, that her story may have been filled with sound and fury, but it ultimately signified nothing; Casey was merely a bad apple.

But what if Casey Anthony was the first of something new and different; an *early adopter of emerging technology*. Someone so determined to break the shackles of personal responsibility and social expectation that she violently rebelled against an archaic system...yes, there was blood, but this is rebellion; this was a statement, and in ten years, young adults may look back at the courageous Casey Anthony as a forerunner of after-birth abortion...after all, she didn't feel like being a mother anymore, so she broke up with it; it was an integrity move.

Feel good scolding Casey Anthony, queen villain, from your godly throne at your computer. Perfect son of God, ten years later—still chasing women on dating apps, using the right words in the right order to get to the end of the game—rest easy knowing Casey Anthony is entirely unlike you.

[10] In nearly every conversation about Jodi Arias' murder of Travis Alexander, after everyone agrees that murder is *awful* and *unjustifiable*, it's inevitably mentioned that Travis was "only using Jodi for sex," while Arias desperately chased commitment from him, and that soundbite is left alone to hang in the air.

This transforms the Arias murder from something binary—she stabbed a naked man 30 times, slit his throat, and shot him in the head and therefore is aggressively guilty—to a nuanced matter of her *degrees of guilt*. Lifetime even made a movie about Arias which served as thinly veiled revenge porn; Lifetime, the *network for women*. We're supposed to understand the Arias case as *two wrongs;* which is more wrong only depends on your perspective. Lifetime's perspective is immediately apparent in the film's title: *Dirty Little Secret* (2013), a reference to their relationship, not the murder.

No. Women don't understand the word "no."

[11] She always hated Nancy; she thought Nancy was *cursed*. Not exactly a wholly inaccurate suspicion based on past history, but one more rooted in cultural tradition, or so I had thought. *The Angel of Death;* we joked that dating Nancy would eventually would kill me—a black widow kind of thing, something never too unwelcome—let Nancy fuck me to death, I'd tell her. Dark humor would get us through the day. That summer, her boyfriend killed himself. Suddenly things weren't so funny. She was sent home from work that day and her job had cookies delivered. This is how corporate America responds to tragedy. She blamed Nancy for this, implying some kind of transference of destinies, or that maybe spiritual lines were crossed. I could never tell if she was kidding, making light of something that was silently destroying her. The long empty nights, the nightmares she'll never share. My secret loser Internet friend. *The Happy Phantom:* we never met in person, and maybe never will, but we shared moments that were real and unforgettable. I don't know if I was there for her in the way I should have been, but she told me that this passage made her cry, made the pain a little easier to bear, and I'm grateful for that. When Nancy and I broke up, she insisted that I seek out a priest. Spiritually cleanse. Don't pass on curse, okay?

[12] *Incest with My Little Sister Who is Hospitalized Repeatedly: Today, I Saw the Sea. I'm No Longer Afraid.*

[13] *The Lady's Dressing Room* (1732).

[14] "How would I describe myself? Three words: hardworking, alpha male, jackhammer, merciless, insatiable." Dwight is the butt of jokes on the first

few seasons of *The Office* (2005) based on this simple dynamic: people don't like unattractive men having masculine attributes; it's perceived as unearned confidence and is used as a basis for ridicule.

[15] A similar dynamic exists between Josh and corporate boss MacMillan, a toy company veteran who is sick of working with joyless and ineffective corporate drones. MacMillan appreciates Josh's childlike sincerity and enthusiasm, promoting him to the top of the company, while willfully ignoring the rather obvious red flags of Josh's immaturity…imposing his own narrative on Josh.

[16] When my kid girlfriend and I broke up, I was entrenched in this bizarre combination of heartbreak and relief. Another reason to avoid large age gaps: you inevitably end up taking on the role of caretaker or surrogate parent, and letting go of that can feel strange. Around this time, I rewatched *Big* (1988) and was surprised by how much I related to Susan's story, of imposing a pervasive narrative on someone else as a way of filling in the gaps and seeing what you want. The kid was over things the day they ended, and isn't that how it was always going to go?

[17] *Mrs. Doubtfire* (1993) is absolutely insane, and anyone who follows the narrative as intended is equally insane…or am I being pretentious and judgmental for thinking critically about a family comedy from the early 90's?

[18] Pearl Jam had their own audience-shedding record around this time with *Vitalogy* (1993)—initially released exclusively on vinyl for two weeks before the CD and cassette became available, containing angry yet rockin' songs like "Not for You" and "Spin the Black Circle"—Pearl Jam refused to commit as deeply as Nirvana and Green Day in shaking out the frat house crowd, still including a "blatantly great pop song" in "Better Man," a song which the band was hesitant to record due to its "accessibility" (via *Spin*, Vol.17, No.8 [2001]).

[19] Bush, an English grunge band who were outsiders to the American culture of self-conscious self-hatred, decided to make their own *dark* and *difficult* album—assuming it was just the thing to do—following their massively successful debut, *Sixteen Stone* (1994), which boasted a remarkable five hit singles. Bush hired *In Utero*'s Steve Albini and promptly

removed everything that made their debut radio-friendly. *Razorblade Suitcase* (1996) is an aural manifestation of Bush following trends into the witches' oven, and unlike their American counterparts, they didn't get the joke; failing to include just enough *incidental* good shit to squeeze a *reluctant* hit single, Bush fully committed to making an awful record and effectively tanked their band. There's a purity to this.

[20] Wheels burning pavement at 5AM—if "Learn to Fly" hits the playlist, I know I'll have to remember to clean up before going in—even if I'm the only one there. If you were a part of the right mixing board and happened to be following along—on the right signal; tuned into the right frequency, with your AM radio set just right—the death of Sky King Rich affected you in ways still difficult to find terms for three years later. Men who were strangers outside of anonymous Twitter handles inexplicably arriving at the same emotional conclusions; the feeling of *deep shit*, on the bench outside the principal's office with the large analog clock perched above, audible clicking as sharp as the blade of a guillotine. Anyone whose life had brought them to the same, immediate, *a priori* understanding of how and why the Sky King came to be was, at the same time, gutted by the event in ways that would be confusing for anyone on the outside looking in. Reminding myself aloud to wipe away tears before walking into work—at work, certainly no one would understand the pain of having nothing to live for, nothing to strive for, nothing worth dying for—*looking to the sky to save me, looking for a sign of life, looking for something to help me burn out bright*...no one outside of us could understand the quiet desperation, the strange mixture of admiration and grief, the daydreaming fantasies of using Rich as an avatar, like a kid in 1977 imagining himself to be Gene Simmons, tongue wagging in the mirror, red food coloring running down his neck and staining his mother's soft pink, shag bathroom rug. Unfair to use a stranger's suicide as a halfhearted immature wish fulfillment, but the problem was ultimately recursive—the Sky King's death was caused by the same elements that made the Sky King appealing as a fantasy—a fantasy, in part, because we never truly knew Rich outside of his final moments, whose audio was preserved. Rich's final moments, chock full of the same dark humor and nihilistic charisma that people entrenched in Internet culture call shitposting—Rich facing his last moments with admirable courage—had one moment of hesitation, a moment that stuck with me, and one that immediately comes to mind when "Learn to Fly" hits the

playlist; *not quite ready to bring it down just yet,* and this is the moment that haunts me when I think of the Sky King.[a]

> a. Gio Pennacchietti, landscape and expressionist painter from Ontario, Canada (follow on Twitter at @GiantGio) did two absolutely beautiful paintings of Sky King Rich in flight, both available as prints, one of which I am proud to own.

[21] The heart of masculinity is a man's relationship with power: his efficiency in acquiring power, his comfort in holding power, and his ability to maintain power. This is the core of masculinity, the Platonic form of masculinity. There may be markers or signifiers that point toward this— usually these signifiers are mistakenly understood as masculinity itself— but they only aid in coming to understand an individual's relationship with power.

[22] A Time to Talk

When a friend calls to me from the road

And slows his horse to a meaning walk,

I don't stand still and look around

On all the hills I haven't hoed,

And shout from where I am, "What is it?"

No, not as there is a time to talk.

I thrust my hoe in the mellow ground,

Blade-end up and five feet tall,

And plod: I go up to the stone wall

For a friendly visit.

[23] Kratom is the darling miracle drug of the self-improvement community. "I credit kratom for helping me to accomplish just about everything I've achieved in the past six years," explains a popular Internet guru. "Unlike many natural dietary supplements that do nothing, kratom can seriously help anxiety, depression, addiction, motivation, sleep, etc.

"Kratom works by stimulating your opiate receptors. It has 'opiate-like' effects. However, kratom is NOT an opiate...this is what makes kratom far safer than all other 'opiates' that are addicting and subject to overdose... less 'lethal' than alcohol and even Tylenol, which kills almost 1,000 people a year."

[24] *Not Dead and Not for Sale* (2011).

[25] This particular summer felt like a rebirth—detoxing from kratom forced me to spend a lot of time alone, and the RLS had me walking seven to ten miles daily just to tire my legs out enough to get a few hours of sleep—long walks, alone, from early evening into the night, meditative and soul-cleansing. Time I recall fondly.

[26] I wanted to start the story with a number doubling for the name of a character—cold and impersonal—pointing to how inorganic and data-driven life had become; everybody as a statistic, everybody as a tiny piece of the algorithm, everybody as a little consumer.

[27] I always loved Pynchon's ability to draw the reader's attention to the *language* of a story. I would not have written this book had I not read *The Crying of Lot 49* (1965) as a college sophomore. I wanted a lot of the language for "In the Bedroom" to be ambiguous and disconnected from meaning; hopefully, phrases like *almost lively* convey this sense, ultimately conveying nothing at all.

[28] Along with language disconnected from meaning, I wanted the story to be full of other missed connections rendering things meaningless. Kristen and Ten are playing Scrabble without a game board; later, they have sex while Ten watches MTV.

[29] "Bada, ba ba ba" always sounded like baby talk to me, or a kind of *pre-language*. Emerging from this state, the others skip right to the intended corporate slogan, with nothing in-between and nothing organic, while Kat gets it wrong; another missed connection.

[30] *Fangoria* No. 62 (1987).

[31] Follow me on Twitter at @KillToParty.

[32] Growing up from the very depths of 1980's pop culture, a child will take

for granted the idea that every bit of entertainment devised in Hollywood laboratories by mad scientist writers will deliver as promised, in comedic, action-soaked brilliance. Every bit of media better than the next, a neverending ladder being built in real time that will someday, in the distant future, touch the face of God. This is true consumer innocence, and once it's lost, it's gone for good. Watching *Ghostbusters II* (1989) in theaters, the week of its release, was that moment for me; where, like Thomas doubting his own eyes, I made my father take me back to the theater the very next weekend for a second go-around. I must have missed something; I must be in the wrong, I thought, not Hollywood, not *my friends* Dan Aykroyd and Bill Murray; they would never betray my trust. It was leaving the mall theater that second time, with my father, that I realized that yes, sometimes things can suck.

[33] Follow me on Twitter at @KillToParty.

[34] A corporate slogan; hollow language disconnected from meaning, ultimately saying nothing.

[35] "Look, boy, either Michael Jackson is some guy working in a recording studio in L.A. or he's here with you willing to work on this song. It's your choice."

[36] *Missing Richard Simmons* (2017).

[37] I'm so sorry, Bruiser.

[38] Isn't that right, Holden?

[39] From "In Pursuit of Lolita" (*Vanity Fair* [July 1986]), and also used as a selling-point blurb on the cover of the 1997 edition of *Lolita* (1955), notorious in its horrifying inaccuracy for the sake of controversy. Humbert doesn't love Dolores any more than one can love a piece of fiction inspired by a photograph, speaking of his mother in the same reductionary terms: "(picnic, lightning)."

[40] Similarly, people saw what they wanted in this essay, despite deliberately writing it as an anti-brag. No one starving wants to hear a fish story, no matter the size of the catch.

[41] KISS exists as the ultimate symbol disconnected from meaning,

ultimately symbolizing nothing.

[42] *The Secret History of Star Wars* (2008).

[43] Her real number is unknowable, a Platonic form; only a close approximation is possible.

[44] I always share my essays with the women who appear in them; implant lady decided to leave a comment on my blog, which, in the spirit of fairness, I will include here:

"You 1000% write for attention otherwise you would of [sic] never texted me this link to read this shit. You use big words to feel good about yourself and you use your meaningless experiences with women that you meet that are probably in every sense of the word to [sic] good for you. So keep writing about your extremely exaggerated experiences hoping one day someone will read this and give you a shot at something more. Hahaha.

"Good luck!

"Oh and my tits look amazing you only wish you got to see them."

[45] Rewatching *Return of the Jedi* (1983) as an adult makes the scene where Luke burns the body of his father stand out as the true climax of the original trilogy; the culmination of Luke's journey. While it may seem tragic that sister Leia wasn't there beside him, this was something Luke had to do alone. After all, it was only Luke who saw the human face of his father and bore witness to his humanity; only Luke would have been able to *understand* his father. Luke delivering his father's funeral was his final rite of passage into manhood and the true return of the Jedi.

Every man will have to bury his father, but will every man have understood his father when the time comes? The evolution of a man's relationship with his father mirrors Luke's struggle with Darth Vader throughout the course of the *Star Wars* saga, from not truly knowing him through the inevitable conflict of a young man's transition to adulthood. If you're lucky, you'll have a moment where the pieces come together and you see your father as a part of yourself, but not everyone gets there…and, unlike a Hollywood movie, the story may end first.

Luke learning his father was Darth Vader, galactic overlord, was shocking enough to cause a suicide attempt. The perceived failing of his father was more important to Luke than Vader's *identity* as father. Culturally, we understand men primarily through the contributions which they offer; only women are bestowed with inherent social value. Vader failed Luke by virtue of running the Empire—to silly Luke, this was the antithesis of value—and thus invalidated Vader's status as a father to him.

Of course, you would have jumped at the chance to "rule the galaxy together as father and son," but Luke was a stupid motherfucker.

Our modern conception of fatherhood may be less dramatic, but it's not very different. When a respect for fatherhood isn't something institutionalized—ours is a world where *Father Knows Best* (1954) is treated like a bad joke—we default to a father only being worth what he's able to contribute. Problematically, this contribution is judged by those who may not be old enough to understand the bigger picture: the reason why unpopular decisions are necessary.

Women raise children, and men raise adults. The connection a child has to their mother is drastically different than the relationship developed with their father. Like a woman's social value, the relationship she has with her children is inherent, bestowed by nature. Biologically, a man is a sperm donor; fatherhood is a *social construct*.

So it follows that a boy will first get to know his father through the lens of his mother. The purpose of the patriarchy as a familial structure wasn't male dominance through brute force, having women relegated to a role between sex slave and housekeeper, but rather as way to guarantee that fathers wouldn't be excluded.

The expectation for a wife was to have respect for her husband—"for better, for worse, for richer, for poorer, in sickness and in health"—in our modern world it seems appropriate, and rather pressing, to add "in times of strength" and "moments of weakness."

The father you knew wasn't the man who attracted your mother; attracting a woman is the easy part. You put your best foot forward; you accentuate the positives and hide the negatives, you do everything in your power to embody the fantasy she has of the *perfect man*. It isn't an act—this man is someone you'd like to be, and her attraction makes you feel confident in that identity—you strive to be her rock.

But life is hard, and every man will stumble; he'll feel defeated, he'll question himself, and he'll find it increasingly difficult to hide these feelings from his wife. When respect was her responsibility, it may have encouraged him to fight, but in the wild west of a post-patriarchy, she'll more likely resent any sign of weakness. In the dance of mating and courtship, women are those who select, and she'll be irritated thinking she chose a buffoon. In a world where divorce is an easy escape, she'll wonder *what if*.

I remember standing next to the eggs at the supermarket with my mom when I was twelve. We ran into my best friend's mom. She was buying eggs, too. They got to chatting, and within a minute or so, she tells my mom that she never wanted to marry my friend's dad—he was a good guy, but he was boring—he was her back-up plan. Her main choice wasn't interested, but now she wonders *what if*. Then we picked out our eggs and went to the checkout.

In all fairness, the guy was seriously boring.

The father you met was a man who had been through a lot; was the mother you had the type to respect him through his struggles, or wonder *what if?*

Maybe I'm a cynic, but *Welcome to Hell* (2021), where a son's perception of his father will be tainted by his mother's disappointment. As a teenager, and the inevitable conflict inherent to those years, a poor foundation for this relationship will only worsen. If you think your father is a weak loser, suddenly a weak loser is telling you what you can and can't do, for reasons that aren't immediately apparent.

And that's if your father hasn't checked out entirely.

Shaping the image of your father through the eyes of your mother created a man only worth what he could do for you. His failings became magnified; you defined him through his shortcomings. As implicit as these feelings may have been, they seeped into the cracks of your relationship and weakened it. This may have further damaged a man already struggling to be the father and husband he needed to be.

You surely had a moment, as a young adult, where you saw parts of him in yourself and were horrified—like Luke in *The Empire Strikes Back* (1980), when he sees his own face in Vader's mask—you experienced the fear of becoming your father. This was something you wanted to fight against. Your father was a weak man; your father was the villain.

I remember when I first saw things in my father that my mother couldn't see, maybe things my father, himself, couldn't understand. As I got older, I became more in touch with what was lurking under the surface of particular emotions; *why* I felt the way I felt. The insecurities, the sadness, the self-doubt. A marker for adulthood may be understanding the true challenge of adulthood: understanding that a man's life is defined by struggle.

Take a moment to recognize that your father was alone in that struggle. He didn't have the connectivity and resources of modern technology which has served to foster a re-emergence of masculinity and an understanding of gender dynamics. He was taught that his generation embodied a *better way of thinking,* and a good man was one who embraced this progression. Gone was the responsibility to lead a relationship; his generation embraced an *equal partnership.* A good man was a compassionate man who respected his wife's strength and independence, and in turn, she would forgive his moments of failure and weakness.

Just like you, all your father wanted was to be a good man.

And as this way of thinking slowly destroyed him, it was all he knew.

When Luke looks down at his robotic hand, reminiscent of his robotic father, after striking him down as the Emperor cackles, he finally *gets it.* Life is hard, and Vader was only a man, not an impossible ideal to embody, nor a man only worth the sum of his contributions. Vader was a man, like Luke, and a man only Luke could understand; if not for Luke's empathy and compassion, Vader was alone in the galaxy.

It may not be as dramatic, but it's just as heroic: your father only has you.

[46] This is not true; you couldn't use a pencil in space, as a bit of broken graphite may damage instruments, but the lie is more captivating than the

truth.

[47] Well, theoretically...

[48] Books sales this, Twitter followers that. *It should be you.* How could she think of shit like that during sex? She's not in the moment.

[49] Venom's *Welcome to Hell* (1981) served as the world's first black metal album; unintentionally, of course, as musical genres tend to manifest spontaneously, organically, in a flow state stemming from the unconscious mind of patient zero and will begin taking on a life of their own, concurrently serving to define the original artist's style and legacy. Welcome to Hell was the blueprint: hypnotic repeating riffs, vocals buried in the mix, lyrics with Satanic imagery, rough production, and songs abruptly cutting in and out. This was partially incidental, however; *Welcome to Hell* was only meant to be a demo tape, which the record company—who didn't want to spend money on a rerecording—thought was good enough to be released as a proper album.

Venom was happy to imbue their sophomore effort, *Black Metal* (1982) with tighter production, but it didn't matter much; the roadmap had been written. When Quorthon released the self-titled *Bathory* (1984) debut, it may as well have been Venom fan-fiction with riffs and song-titles stolen; some modified, some whole cloth. Quorthon retained Venom's incidental low-fi production, doubled-down on the hypnotic repeating riffs, and added the abrasive screeching vocal style that has become a genre staple.

When Mayhem emerged, they were a conglomerate of the two—lifting Venom's album title to formalize the movement and choosing a band name that seemed appropriate—*Mayhem* was a keyword used by both of Euronymous' influences. Other less obvious theft is there if you look for it: Mayhem's excellent *Live in Leipzig* (1993), whose terrible cassette-deck-in-the-back-of-the-club sound quality only added to its charm, wouldn't exist if not for Venom's dog-shit sounding cash-in *Official Bootleg* (1986), on which Chronos assured the audience they'd have a night of "pure fucking mayhem"; "Pure Fucking Armageddon" became the last track of Mayhem's debut record *Deathcrush* (1987). Even theoretical purist Varg Vikernes wasn't above all the shameless theft; several riffs on his debut album,

Burzum (1992), sound suspiciously familiar, as suspiciously familiar as Vikernes' own career trajectory was to hero Quorthon. From the middle of the decade moving forward, most black metal bands existed as some combination of first-wave acts who themselves were busy ripping off Venom, Bathory...and KISS; yes, even the introduction of *corpse paint* has dubious origins.

Which is when you realize there are no more fairy tales; there is no purity; nothing is authentic. Everything is derivative; copies of copies, each fading a bit from the last, only slight modifications made; a crooked signature, a minor personal stamp, none of it resonating. If you can't be one of the greats, why even bother?

You can only ever be derivative of Delicious Tacos; he got there first, sunk his ballpoint spear into virgin soil. There can only ever be *just like Delicious Tacos,* like how it's impossible for any modern president to supersede the historic greats—the Platonic form of *American President,* at least in public consensus—one can only be Lincolnian or *Washington-esque.* The Velvet Underground set the mold for alternative rock, something Kurt Cobain must have intrinsically knew when he blew his head off; *why even bother?*

Why even bother when Houellebecq was writing about the cursed singles-market of the current year, 20 years early; all of it presciently described by Houellebecq when you were still fumbling with bra straps and falling in love. All of it, regurgitated Houellebecq; you could only ever hope to be Houellebecqian. *Why even bother?*

Why bother when even the greats—the historically significant, a class you will never sit with—have an expiration date? Green Day put out their best work—genre defining pop punk, albums that still hit hard 30 years later—as vomit-soaked teenagers. Now, with the wisdom of age and the maturity of adulthood, they write garbage. Metallica peaked with their first five records, and even after learning the hard lesson that chasing fame will only lead to destruction, they were never able to reclaim their creative edge; their last 20 years of material, the majority of the band's existence, have been decent work but nothing earthshattering. nothing historically significant. Had Kurt Cobain lived, he'd almost certainly be embarrassing himself by now.

Why even bother; let the perfect get in the way of the good. Jeff Gutt cashing checks—why even bother when this isn't his story and it never could be—filler songs on forgotten albums.

Every girl is a little more derivative than the last; every moment shared a cheap imitation of that morning, before homeroom, that hung in the air like an eternal sunrise. Why even bother—this is your rock star reunion tour for a band that never caught on in the first place—you *ain't had no prime*. But now you're falling apart and trying to cash in anyway. Derivative garbage; a disingenuous cope. You can't write your way out of this one, bucko, but keep trying. *Why even bother?*

Why even bother when it's all a big nothing; only death is real. You missed your chance to have a story and the best you can do is to pretend it's okay. Good luck with that, loser.

***

Tony Soprano dies at the end, but not before completing his story arc as a conclusion to the show's hypothesis: is it "all a big nothing?" Something his mother lived and died believing. It was popular to say that the ending of *The Sopranos* (2007) was bullshit—that it had no definitive conclusion; that David Chase had devised the finale as a way to frustrate the audience; an elaborate prank; a bizarre, big-budget troll—but like anything they've ever said, the polar opposite is true: *The Sopranos* concludes with Tony realizing that life is made up of a series of tiny moments, half-seconds further halved; moments so brief that you may be the only one to ever notice. That the past weighs us down and the future hasn't yet been written—each a distraction; a vicious mind-eraser; a psychic vampire—each a distraction from these little moments; from our ability to *focus on the good times*.

Life is series of precious moments, and it's up to you to decide what to do with them; Quorthon being influenced by his favorite band; Varg Vikernes following in the footsteps of his hero; Jeff Gutt writing the best record he can, because now is his time and he's going to make every fucking second count. This is his story.

The New York Dolls, genre defining pioneers of proto-punk along with Lou Reed, reunited after 30 years apart for a record and a tour. Too easy to call bullshit on yet another big-name rock reunion; *why even bother* when their artistic prime had already peaked, when any new material produced could never hope to eclipse their best; the Platonic form; what's etched into the hollows of time and the rock-and-roll pantheon; what's historically significant; *why even bother,* something Reed surely would have understood when he attempted career suicide.

Why even bother, something the Dolls addressed with the title of their reunion album, *One Day it Will Please Us to Remember Even This* (2006). The Dolls didn't give a damn that something new couldn't hope to compete with their best; who the fuck cares? This was their story, this was their moment, and every moment counts—this was their time—and their story wasn't over.

ABOUT THE AUTHOR

"Bad" Billy Pratt lives in his hometown of Elk Cove, Oregon with his girlfriend Gertie. Vowing to bring the "wonders of the world" to the people of Elk Cove, he created the "Wonders of the World" miniature golf course with his friends Dean and Annie. *Welcome to Hell* is his first book. Billy writes at *KillToParty.com* and can be reached at BadBillyPratt@protonmail.com or via Twitter at @KillToParty.

terrorhousepress.com

Made in the USA
Monee, IL
27 October 2024